AIMING FOR AN A IN A-LEVEL BUSINESS

Philip Waterhouse

HODDER
EDUCATION
AN HACHETTE UK COMPANY

Although every effort has been made to ensure that website addresses are correct at time of going to press, Hodder Education cannot be held responsible for the content of any website mentioned in this book. It is sometimes possible to find a relocated web page by typing in the address of the home page for a website in the URL window of your browser.

Hachette UK's policy is to use papers that are natural, renewable and recyclable products and made from wood grown in sustainable forests. The logging and manufacturing processes are expected to conform to the environmental regulations of the country of origin.

Orders: please contact Bookpoint Ltd, 130 Park Drive, Milton Park, Abingdon, Oxon OX14 4SE. Telephone: (44) 01235 827827. Fax: (44) 01235 400401. Email education@bookpoint.co.uk Lines are open from 9 a.m. to 5 p.m., Monday to Saturday, with a 24-hour message answering service. You can also order through our website: www.hoddereducation.co.uk

ISBN: 978 1 5104 2414 2

© Philip Waterhouse 2018

First published in 2018 by

Hodder Education,

An Hachette UK Company

Carmelite House

50 Victoria Embankment

London EC4Y 0DZ

www.hoddereducation.co.uk

Impression number	10 9 8 7 6 5 4 3 2 1				
Year	2022	2021	2020	2019	2018

Typeset by Integra Software Services Pvt. Ltd., Pondicherry, India

Printed in Spain

A catalogue record for this title is available from the British Library.

Contents

Getting the most from this book

Aiming for an A is designed to help you master the skills you need to achieve the highest grades. The following features will help you get the most from this book:

Learning objectives

> A summary of the skills that will be covered in the chapter.

 Exam tip

Practical advice about how to apply your skills to the exam.

Activity

An opportunity to test your skills with practical activities.

! Common pitfall

Problem areas where candidates often miss out on marks.

Annotated example

Exemplar answers with commentary showing how to achieve top grades.

Worked example

Step-by-step examples to help you master the skills needed for top grades.

You should know

> A summary of key points to take away from the chapter.

About this book

The aim of this book, just like that of a successful business, needs to be clearly stated at the very start. In a competitive marketplace, the need to have a USP (unique selling point) and differentiate yourself from the competition is very important. There are a range of revision guides for business on the market — but what makes this one stand out? The focus of this guide is on helping you master the key skills you need to access the highest grades possible. This will allow you not only to gain entry to a top-level university, but also to have an A* or A grade on your future CV.

One of the best aspects of studying business is that you can link what you learn in class to pretty much any situation. A simple walk down your local high street, catching up on a current news story, choosing your new phone — these can all be related back to your studies. As you work through your course, you should be aiming to link what you learn in the classroom to what is happening around you.

Your starting base of knowledge is not, however, what will ultimately help you gain an A. Rather, your approach towards study, study skills and determination to continually improve upon your work will be the key to your success. So, what is required to get a top grade in business?

Grade boundaries

While grade boundaries are subject to change each year, a good starting point is to understand what the previous year's grade boundaries were and the likely number of marks that will see you achieve an A* or A grade. In the table below you can see the raw marks and percentages that were required to achieve the top grades for each exam board.

AQA			Edexcel			OCR			WJEC		
Grade	Marks out of 300	%	Grade	Marks out of 300	%	Grade	Marks out of 240	%	Grade	Marks out of 300	%
A*	220	73	A*	208	69	A*	187	78	A*	181	60
A	195	65	A	187	62	A	167	70	A	163	54
B	166	55	B	158	53	B	142	59	B	139	46
C	137	46	C	130	43	C	117	49	C	115	38

Looking at the table above, you could be forgiven for assuming that achieving a top grade is relatively straightforward. However, as with any business decision, you need to consider a range of other factors. All the exam boards are governed by the JCQ (Joint Council of Qualifications) and so each exam board can only award a similar percentage of the top grades. In the table on page 6 you can see just how many of the top grades are awarded for A-level business across all the exam boards. There are just over 30,000 students taking the subject and the table shows the percentages of overall grades awarded.

Grade	% of grades awarded
A*	3.4%
A	11.8%
B	29.1%
C	30.4%
D	17.3%
E	6.1%

Therefore, while the grade boundaries might seem rather low and easy to access, the simple fact is that to become a top performer, you need to make sure you are in the top 15% of all students taking the subject. In other terms, you must ensure that you are one of the best 4,500 students in the land. The aim of this guide is to give you every help possible to ensure you are in the top 15% — so make sure you are paying attention!

The qualities of an A*/A student

The following features are what you need to be targeting to achieve a top grade:

→ You score highly on the multiple-choice questions (90%+).

→ You demonstrate precise knowledge and understanding and your definitions are accurate and precise.

→ Your calculations are correct and units of measurement are always shown.

→ Your answers are well organised and structured and show evidence of planning.

→ Your responses directly answer the questions asked and fully identify and respond to the hooks in the questions.

→ You use your time effectively and cover all of the questions.

→ You score consistently across all of the questions and papers.

→ You build up your arguments using a clear, logical chain of reasoning and you draw in examples that are relevant and used well.

→ Your essays are well organised, with a clear introduction and a clear conclusion that provides an answer to the question asked.

The 12 rules for success

Before getting into the specifics of each examination skill, there is some general advice that should underpin the whole of your A-level study:

1. Acknowledge that A-level *is* a step up from GCSE. Far more emphasis is placed on the higher-order skills of analysis and evaluation rather than merely knowing key terms. While knowledge acts as a gatekeeper to access the question, more marks are awarded for the response that demonstrates analytical and evaluative content.

2. Remember that this is a 2-year course. You are unlikely to get the best mark in your first essay, and there may be times when a particular topic is difficult to understand. Don't forget you have 2 years of preparation for your final exam.

3. Know what your exam board wants. Know the level descriptors, and spend time reading the questions. If you know exactly what you need to achieve the top grade levels, you are far more likely to hit your target. Approach the exam as you would your driving test. Recognise what the examiners are looking for and deliver answers that fulfil these requirements.

4. Remember that there is not always one 'right' answer. Business involves opinions and the wording of the longer exam questions will always frame the question to give you an opportunity to put forward *your* opinion. While there might be advantages and disadvantages of a particular course of action, ultimately examiners reward you for making a justified judgement, putting forward *your* decision which is based on the arguments you have made.

5. Do *not* sit on the fence. You can express your views and give arguments for and against but you *must* come to a clear final decision.

6. Remember that there is no 'right' way to write an essay. While this guide puts forward some suggested templates, you will need to develop your *own* style as you apply advice, along with tips and hints from feedback that you receive from your teachers. The best essays often do not follow a prescribed stucture. However, they do have a simple common factor — they *clearly answer* the *exact* question asked.

7. Look beyond your lessons. Use input from your friends and their work, and from your teacher. Arguably the least used but most useful resource is the exam board documents on their websites. These include examiner reports, model answers, practice exam papers and mark schemes that will allow you to find out exactly what the examiners are looking for.

8. Reflect. Acknowledge and learn from your mistakes in order to improve.

9. Get feedback on your work. This will give you tailored advice that you can use to identify where you need to improve.

10. Be aware of your sources. Over-reliance on popular websites can lead to very similar and generic responses. You should be aiming to make your response stand out for its originality and its ability to answer directly the question set.

11. Recognise that stating examples won't get you the top marks. It is how you use these examples effectively that will help you achieve the highest grades.

12. Enjoy the subject. If you take a keen interest in what you learn in the classroom and are then able to link this to what happens in the real world, you are likely to increase your understanding even further and this will help you develop your responses effectively.

Your approach

Henry Ford, one of the most successful entrepreneurs of the last century, summed it up rather nicely: 'Whether you think you can, or you think you can't — you're right.'

This means that you need to be approaching your studies with a positive attitude and mindset right from the start. While you might have an interest in the subject, it is going to take time to learn exactly how to structure your responses and make the most of the new models and theories that you are learning about. You might be really keen on cars and learning to drive but you are not going to be able to pass your driving test after just one lesson — and the same applies to A-levels. It is important to understand that achieving success is a journey and a process. You will do well to remember this when the going gets tough, as it inevitably will at times.

The learning-to-drive analogy is a good one to keep in mind during your studies. The likelihood is that one of the most important aspects of your time in sixth form will be passing your test and gaining the freedom that comes from being an independent driver. It is likely that you will put considerable time and effort into not only learning the practical skills to pass the actual test for driving, but also practising numerous theory tests to make sure you get the required pass mark. You should view this guide as you would a learner driver's manual or the highway code. They are probably not your first choice of reading material or of a way to spend your free time. However, they will both hopefully be very useful in helping maximise your chances of success.

The aim of this guide is to inform you of exactly the required skills that examiners are looking for, offer tips on how to structure your responses and give a clear breakdown of how marks are awarded and why. If you can follow the rules and give examiners what they are looking for, then you are clearly on a winning path.

Using this book

Each chapter in this book looks at developing a different skill. Combining these skills is all part of completing the jigsaw that will enable you to access the highest possible grades.

→ Chapter 1 will give you a good outline of the key skills your examiners look for and how you will be assessed. It will help you to understand the 'bigger picture' of the business A-level.

→ Chapter 2 will look at the key numerical skills that you will require for the different calculations that you will be expected to make and interpret in your responses. The A-level business specifications place great significance on these formulae and you will need to become confident in applying them, alongside knowing how to use them to analyse the significance of the answers in relation to the business in question.

→ Chapter 3 will teach you how to read effectively and quickly, and give you advice on what to read to help develop relevant business insight. You will also learn how to make notes that are useful and valuable, both in your lessons and from your reading.

→ Chapter 4 tackles the process of writing short, analytical responses, and how to ensure that you give the examiner exactly what they are looking for. You'll gain advice on how to write these quickly and effectively to maximise your marks in the shortest time.

→ Chapter 5 addresses the wide range of skills involved in writing long essays, from simply understanding the question to writing analytical and evaluative paragraphs, rather than merely being descriptive. It will also illustrate the infrastructure that supports these long essays — planning and structuring them, and reflecting on how to improve your own work.

→ Chapter 6 is for use as your exams approach. It reviews different ways in which you can revise, and more importantly what to do in the exam hall to give you every chance of success.

→ The final section, 'Exam board focus', is a reference for you to understand exactly what is in *your* exam and how you will be assessed, depending on the particular exam board you are studying with. You can pop in and out of this reference section whenever you are trying to understand how your work fits into your overall exam structure.

This book is about refining what you have been learning in class to make sure you are giving the examiner exactly what they are looking for amidst the pressures of the exam hall.

1 Key assessment objectives

Learning outcomes

> To identify the skills that are tested at A-level
> To understand how to demonstrate these skills

The aim of this guide is to help you understand exactly what is required to achieve the highest possible grades in your business qualification. Throughout you will be given ideas, hints, tips and practical advice to maximise your chances of getting the top grades. There will be guidance on the specific skills you will be expected to showcase, and how to go about convincing the examiner that you fully understand what the questions are looking for and how to structure your answers effectively.

The fundamentals for any A-level qualification are based around Bloom's taxonomy and these are the basis of the four key assessment objectives. These are as follows:

→ AO1: Knowledge
→ AO2: Application
→ AO3: Analysis
→ AO4: Evaluation

The relative weightings of these objectives will differ slightly for each exam board but they are each very important in their own way. You should be aware of how to demonstrate these skills from an early stage and develop your mastery of them as you progress through the course. It is important to know that each skill is built upon the one before — essentially they should be seen as building blocks to achieve the highest grades. To access the very highest grades, it is crucial that you master the so-called 'higher-order' skills of analysis and evaluation. However, these cannot be accessed unless you first demonstrate a firm grasp of the key terms from the specification.

What follows is a very brief introduction to what each skill is about. Throughout the guide, we will be returning to these in much more detail.

The key skills
Knowledge

Knowledge is obviously crucial and has always been seen as the 'gatekeeper' for accessing the higher levels of the mark scheme. It has perhaps become even more important now that the qualifications are linear, with all the exams taken at the end —

the linear system means that you can be tested on your subject understanding of key terms from anywhere on the syllabus.

Throughout the course, make a glossary of key terms. This can be done either by traditional pen and paper methods, or by using a computer to build a glossary file. Regularly test yourself and learn the new key terms on a weekly basis. The glossary should be a working document that you continue to add to throughout the course.

Application

Application can be demonstrated in many ways. The main way is showing you understand the context of the question and the business referred to. Another way is to use the data provided and comment on its significance (see Chapter 2, on quantitative skills, for more detail). On the longer, more evaluative questions, you will be given an opportunity to bring in your own examples — it is therefore important to read widely around the subject throughout the course, as will be discussed further in Chapter 3.

> ### ✓ Exam tip
>
> Start with a definition in every response. Look at the wording of the question and underline or highlight the key term within it. Your first sentence should give a clear and precise explanation of what the key term means.

Activity

Aim to build up a bank of examples and case studies that you can use in your answers. While the exam papers will feature specific case studies, the nature of the questions (particularly the longer ones) will mean you are expected to bring in your own examples of businesses that are relevant to a particular business scenario. With this in mind, it would be useful to include in your bank three to four specific businesses from each of the following ten industries that will help you demonstrate application and to compare and contrast with firms that are specifically mentioned in the exam questions themselves:

1. Fashion retail
2. Automotive industry
3. Social media
4. Technology
5. Food retail
6. Mobile phones
7. Gaming consoles
8. Leisure and entertainment
9. Supermarkets
10. Banking and finance

! Common pitfall

Application is not about 'telling a story' or giving a detailed description of a particular business or entrepreneur. It is about choosing a relevant example, naming it in your response and using it to strengthen and develop the argument that you are making. Far too many students try to crowbar in a story they have read about a business, losing focus on the actual question set, then losing relevance, and so failing to gain marks.

Analysis

Analysis is about building up a logical chain of argument that explains the likely cause and effect of a particular action. Good analysis comes from taking a point and developing it into a sustained line of reasoning that answers directly the question set. It is one of the hardest skills to master. When you start building an argument, remember the following rules:

1. Analysis *must* be relevant and stem from the question itself.
2. Build your links slowly and surely and in a logical fashion.
3. Bring back your chain of argument directly to the question set.

The key point with any chain of analysis is that it *must* be linked to the question itself. Examiners are very aware of what is seen as 'generic' analysis that could apply to any business situation and is not directly related to the question. Therefore, to be sure of being awarded the highest levels of response the analysis must be **applied** and **relevant**.

Evaluation

Evaluation is making a supported judgement and deciding about a particular course of action. It is one of the hardest skills to master and is arguably the skill that differentiates students who reach the highest levels from those who achieve an average mark. Your judgement must come from a previous **balanced** set of arguments, but your final decision must be **clear** and **supported**. Make sure you are explaining **why** your decision is the **most** appropriate course of action.

Far too often, students let themselves down by offering a conclusion which is just a summary of previously made points or arguments. This is not high-level evaluation. The key to success is to be opinionated and offer justified reasons why certain courses of action are not as suitable as others. Again, you need to guard against 'generic' judgements that have clearly been pre-learnt.

Throughout this guide we will be returning to these key skills and offering advice and hints on how to develop your mastery further and make sure you are meeting the requirements to achieve that A*/A grade.

The examiner

The examiner is not some 'bogeyman' whom you should be afraid of. In fact, you should be looking at them as a potential future friend whom you want to win over. You can easily find out what they like and dislike as each year they publish an examiner report on the previous year's exam papers. In these documents, you can find out precisely what you need to do on each paper, the rationale behind the wording of the questions, and what examiners are looking for.

Returning to the driving analogy, examiners are similar to the people assessing your ability to drive. They are former or current teachers who appreciate that you are under pressure within the exam hall and that some topics are typically more challenging for students. However, ultimately all any examiner ever expects from you is to specifically answer the question set.

The nature of the exam means that marking can at times be rather subjective and one examiner might view a response as slightly better than another examiner does. However, examiners' work is regularly sampled and monitored, and inconsistent examiners

Activity

A good activity is a 'blowing up the balloon' exercise. Take as many key terms and topics as you can (say 15–20) and try to develop a sustained, logical chain of analysis using connectives such as those from the BLT model: 'Because, Leading to, Therefore'.

✓ Exam tip

The most important factor in evaluation is that your final judgement should *directly* answer the question set. A good tip is to re-read the question again and again as you are writing your response. See Chapter 5 for more on identifying the 'hooks' in a question.

are not allowed to continue marking. The exam boards expect consistency of marking across all of the papers and the correct application of the mark scheme.

The mark schemes that examiners use, similar to the examiner reports, are available to look at. You should be familiar with the previous year's papers and the skills that you are required to demonstrate. All examination boards have moved across to a levelled response approach, with levels broadly as follows:

➜ Level 1: Weak
➜ Level 2: Limited
➜ Level 3: Reasonable
➜ Level 4: Good
➜ Level 5: Excellent

Within each of these levels, the four key assessment objectives are being judged: i.e. knowledge, application, analysis and evaluation. Thus what you are aiming to show the examiner is that your answer is worthy of the highest levels on the mark scheme and is also answering precisely the question set. You will be well on the way to achieving level 4 or 5 as long as your answer:

➜ demonstrates a good understanding of the key terms within the question
➜ is directly focused on the wording of the question
➜ uses relevant examples
➜ builds up a good chain of argument
➜ reaches a clear judgement

As we go through the guide, we will be looking at examples of how all this can be done and why examiners would award top marks. It is worth noting that examiners are actually encouraged to award full marks for a good response (it does not have to be perfect). At the same time, examiners will also operate at the other end of the scale — if there is no evidence of anything of credit, they are likely to award zero.

You should know

> **There are four key assessment objectives to master: knowledge, application, analysis and evaluation.**
> **To access the highest grades, you need to pay special attention to the 'higher-order' skills of analysis and evaluation.**
> **Take an organised, focused approach from day 1 of the course. You will be covering a lot of key content over the 2 years, so making it easy to access will save time in the long run.**
> **Make sure you know how past papers have been marked, and what you can do to reach the highest levels of the mark schemes.**
> **If you answer the question set, use key terms, use relevant examples, build a chain of reasoning and reach a clear judgement, you will be well on your way to a level 4 or 5 response.**

2 Quantitative skills

Learning outcomes

> To recognise the significance of calculations within the A-level
> To know how quantitative skills will be tested and examined
> To be aware of the different calculations and formulae that you need to know
> To know how to prepare for these types of calculations and to understand what kinds of questions might be asked

Numerical handling is a vital skill in all business A-levels and the use of data will be examined in various ways. If you achieved a good grade at GCSE mathematics or an equivalent qualification, the quantitative skills which are tested in the exam should not cause any major problems as they will not involve any challenging mathematics. However, they will need to be practised and an understanding of the business context will be required. You should be viewing the calculations as a way of picking up easy marks.

The use of calculations will form a key test of knowledge (AO1) and you will also be expected to understand the significance of the results of these calculations and how they can be interpreted within a business context. An A*/A candidate should be able to make exact calculations and, more significantly, handle the data to show insight about how the results can be analysed and evaluated, in order to reach the higher levels of the mark schemes.

There are two distinct aspects to the quantitative skills:

→ calculation (AO1)
→ interpretation (AO2, AO3 and AO4)

In the remainder of this chapter, we will look at the various calculations and formulae that you must learn. Note that you will *not* be given a formula sheet in the exams for business (unlike some other A-level subjects), so it is *essential* to learn the formulae. Here we will consider how these may be tested in simple knowledge-based questions and how they may also be tested in relation to particular scenarios, requiring you to use higher-order skills and to build up arguments. The formulae are an integral aspect of the course and it is crucial that you become confident with the different ratios and calculations.

 Exam tip

The calculation questions that test knowledge should represent easy marks to score as a top-level student. They will account for up to 20% of the overall marks in the exam and should be treated as an area where you can showcase your skills. An A*/A student should also be able to handle and interpret the data that are presented.

Marketing maths
Percentage change

You will be familiar with calculating percentages from your GCSE maths studies. However, you also need to be able to apply these calculations to a business context. They form a major part of the marketing maths area of the syllabus.

The following is a good way to calculate percentage change (though you may have been taught a slightly different method):

$$\frac{\text{new value} - \text{old value}}{\text{old value}} \times 100$$

We look next at the use of percentage change calculations in different marketing situations and then at elasticity of demand.

> **✓ Exam tip**
>
> The question will normally indicate how many decimal places you should use in your answer. If it does not, the accepted procedure is to go to 2 decimal places.

Percentage change in marketing scenarios

Below are some examples of how you might be expected to interpret different scenarios and utilise percentage change calculations for different marketing situations.

Worked example 2.1

This first example involves changes in market size (volume).

Calculate the percentage change in quantity of goods and services produced in a particular market over a period of time.

The sales of vinyl records for the UK vinyl record industry increased from 25,000 to 35,000 between May and June.

$$\frac{\text{new value} - \text{old value}}{\text{old value}} \times 100$$

$$\frac{35,000 - 25,000}{25,000} \times 100$$

$$\frac{10,000}{25,000} \times 100 = 40\%$$

Worked example 2.2

Calculate the percentage change in market size (value), i.e. the total sales revenue generated from selling all the goods and services produced in a particular market over a period of time.

The US digital music industry increased in total sales from $4,000 million to $4,500 million between 2013 and 2014.

$$\frac{\text{new value} - \text{old value}}{\text{old value}} \times 100$$

$$\frac{4,500 - 4,000}{4,000} \times 100$$

$$= \frac{500}{4,000} \times 100 = 12.5\%$$

Worked example 2.3

Calculate the percentage change in sales value, i.e. the total sales revenue of a particular business over a period of time.

Sales of CDs at Tesco have decreased from £125 million per annum to £115 million.

$$\frac{\text{new value} - \text{old value}}{\text{old value}} \times 100$$

$$\frac{115 - 125}{125} \times 100$$

$$= \frac{-10}{125} \times 100 = -8\%$$

Worked example 2.4

Calculate the market growth percentage in a particular year 'X', i.e. the percentage change in the size of the market between one year and another.

Sales of vinyl records in the UK increased from just 200,000 to 1.2 million between 2005 and 2015.

$$\frac{\text{new value} - \text{old value}}{\text{old value}} \times 100$$

$$\frac{1.2 - 0.2}{0.2} \times 100$$

$$= \frac{1}{0.2} \times 100 = 500\%$$

Worked example 2.5

Calculate the sales growth percentage in a particular year 'X', i.e. the percentage change in sales of one firm between one year and another.

Sales of headphones for a particular company increased from 7.8 million in 2015 to 12 million in 2016.

$$\frac{\text{new value} - \text{old value}}{\text{old value}} \times 100$$

$$\frac{12 - 7.8}{7.8} \times 100$$

$$= \frac{4.2}{7.8} \times 100 = 53.85\%$$

Worked example 2.6

Calculate the percentage market share of a firm/product/brand at a particular point in time, i.e. the sales of one business OR product OR brand divided by the total sales within that area.

The global music industry has seen its revenues fall by 3% to $15 billion in the previous year. The independent music labels account for $2.2 billion of this total. Calculate their market share.

This is a slightly different calculation — you simply need to divide the sales of the independent sector by the total sales:

$$\frac{2.2}{15} \times 100 = 14.67\%$$

Interpreting the data

From the above worked examples focused on the music industry, you should be able to glean some insights and application to allow you to analyse and develop your responses into stronger lines of argument. So what is happening?

→ Vinyl records are a significantly growing market.

→ Digital and streaming services are growing and making up a larger proportion of the overall market.

→ CD sales are in decline.

→ The accessory market is growing.

→ Overall music sales are in decline.

Picking up on these themes and the likely impact on different stakeholders within the industry can lead to good application and analysis. HMV has had to retrench as it failed to anticipate and react to the move away from physical to digital. Supermarkets like Tesco have introduced vinyl records and accessories as they have reacted to the growing demand. Recording artists have looked to play live more often because sales from their music are in decline as customers stream music instead.

Elasticity of demand

This area often causes difficulties and always acts as a strong discriminator between grades. Because of this, it is frequently examined and offers a great opportunity for scoring well if you can master the concept. The name itself can cause confusion and perhaps a better word than 'elasticity' is '**sensitivity**', as we are measuring how sensitive demand is to a change in price or income:

→ If the figure for elasticity is **greater than 1**, we say it is **elastic or sensitive**.

→ If the figure is **less than 1**, we say it is **inelastic or insensitive**.

These figures are very important as they give firms crucial information about their customers and what they should do.

The formula for **price elasticity of demand (PED)** is as follows:

$$\text{price elasticity of demand} = \frac{\text{percentage change in quantity demanded}}{\text{percentage change in price}}$$

 Exam tip

The numbers used in an exam question are chosen for a reason rather than being randomly selected. They are offering stronger students an opportunity to interpret the significance of the final answer and then build an argument from this. Normally your first answer is right. Trust your instinct and check whether the answer looks suitable or realistic for the case study.

✓ **Exam tip**

It is very easy under the pressure of an exam to miscalculate by putting the equation upside down. Try and use a mnemonic to remember which way around it goes, such as QPR (Queens Park Rangers) for PED — quantity on top, price on the bottom.

For PED the answer will *always* be negative.

The size of the elasticity co-efficient has a major significance for the revenue that a firm can achieve:

→ If the figure (ignoring the minus sign) is greater than 1, it means that the good is price elastic. Therefore the firm will see a significant increase in revenue if it **lowers** the price, as customers are sensitive to price changes and will buy in significantly larger quantities.

→ If the figure is less than 1, it means that the good is price inelastic. Therefore the firm can increase its revenue by **raising** the price, as customers are not sensitive to price changes — while demand will fall, it will not do so by a significant amount and so extra revenue can be earned.

The formula for **income elasticity of demand (YED)** is as follows:

$$\text{income elasticity of demand} = \frac{\text{percentage change in quantity demanded}}{\text{percentage change in income}}$$

For YED the answer will be positive for **normal** goods but negative for **inferior** goods.

The three major influences on the elasticity of a product are as follows:

→ the number of substitutes available
→ the percentage of income spent on the good
→ the degree of need for the good

Again, the type of product will dictate its elasticity and so recognising goods that follow the normal pattern of a positive relationship between income and demand is important — just as it is to spot the cases where demand will have an inverse relationship with income. Again, recognising just how sensitive the product is will help with your analysis.

> ✓ **Exam tip**
>
> Be prepared to comment on the significance of the elasticity co-efficient for the revenue a firm can achieve, in order to show higher levels of analysis.

Worked example 2.7

Ski holiday companies know that if they lower their average price from £1,000 to £900, demand will increase from 1,000 holidays a week to 1,500 holidays a week.

% change in quantity demanded:

$$\frac{\text{new value} - \text{old value}}{\text{old value}} \times 100$$

$$\frac{1,500 - 1,000}{1,000} \times 100$$

$$= \frac{500}{1,000} \times 100 = 50\%$$

% change in price:

$$\frac{\text{new value} - \text{old value}}{\text{old value}} \times 100$$

$$\frac{900 - 1{,}000}{1{,}000} \times 100$$

$$= \frac{-100}{1{,}000} \times 100 = -10\%$$

PED:

$$\frac{\text{percentage change in quantity demanded}}{\text{percentage change in price}}$$

$$\frac{+50\%}{-10\%} = -5 = \text{highly elastic and sensitive}$$

Linking back to revenue:

old revenue = £1,000 × 1,000 = £1 million

new revenue = £900 × 1,500 = £1.35 million

Clearly, the ski holiday company has benefited from reducing the price and substantially increased its revenue.

Interpreting the data

So what is happening within the ski industry and how can individual firms benefit from these calculations?

As ski holidays are considered a luxury and cost a significant percentage of an individual's income, you would expect them to be sensitive to price changes. It is also worth considering that customers have a lot of rival companies to choose from when looking at the potential options for ski holidays. Therefore, companies can use this information to price their holidays accordingly, knowing that a slight cut in the price of their holidays will lead to a significant increase in the demand.

Key financial calculations
Profit and cost

In the previous section on elasticity there was a calculation that involved working out the revenue of a firm. This is a fundamental part of the syllabus and a measurement of the performance of a firm; it forms a major part of the profit calculations that you will be expected to perform. There are various ways in which you will be expected to calculate profits. The formulae are provided in Table 2.1 on page 20.

Table 2.1 Formulae for calculating profit and cost

profit = total revenue − total costs OR profit = total contribution − fixed costs
total costs = fixed costs + variable costs
variable costs = variable cost per unit × number of units sold
total revenue (aka sales revenue, aka turnover) = selling price per unit × number of units sold
gross profit = sales revenue − cost of sales
profit from operations = operating profit = sales revenue − cost of sales − operating expenses
profit for year = operating profit + profit from other activities
contribution per unit = selling price − variable costs per unit
total contribution = contribution per unit × number of units sold OR total contribution = total revenue − total variable costs

Worked example 2.8

A mobile burger van business is looking to set up and run a stall during a music festival. The fixed cost of a pitch at the festival is £3,000 for all 3 days. The business aims to sell 2,000 burgers at £5 each during the festival and each burger costs £1 to make. There are other fixed costs in terms of staffing which amount to £1,500 for the 3 days.

total revenue = 2,000 × £5 = £10,000

total variable costs = £2,000 × £1 = £2,000

total fixed costs = £3,000 + £1,500 = £4,500

profit = £10,000 − £6,500 = £3,500

gross profit = £10,000 − £2,000 = £8,000

contribution per unit = £5 − £1 = £4 per unit

total contribution = £4 per unit × 2,000 = £8,000

OR total contribution = £10,000 − £2,000 = £8,000

Interpreting the data

So is it a good idea for the firm to plan to set up at the festival? What are your reasons? Is there anything else you would need to know? Are any important data missing?

Looking at the figures above, it seems as though the festival option is nicely profitable. However, it needs to be considered that the business is likely to be highly seasonal and the projected sales figures are purely estimates and can't be relied on fully. In addition, the level of competition at a festival from other food vendors is likely to be high and making your food stand out from the other stalls will be difficult.

On the plus side, the mobile burger van can probably face more price inelastic demand as festival goers need to eat. However, the pricing must be in line with that of the other food stalls. If the business could operate at numerous festivals throughout the summer, then this could be a good venture — but the business would need to consider other options out of season.

Break-even and margin of safety

The mobile burger van example can also incorporate another set of very relevant and useful calculations — those of break-even and margin of safety. The **formula for break-even** is as follows:

$$\text{break-even output} = \frac{\text{fixed costs}}{\text{contribution per unit}}$$

This is a crucial formula that you should become very confident with. While break-even can be examined in many other ways, this calculation always works and acts as a check that you are on the right lines.

Alternative calculations are as follows.

On a break-even chart, the break-even output is the level of output at which:

total revenue = total costs

On a break-even chart, the level of profit at a given level of output is the vertical distance between the total revenue line and the total cost line.

The **formula for margin of safety** is as follows:

margin of safety = actual level of output – break-even level of output

Worked example 2.9

Using the mobile burger van example:

$$\text{break-even output} = \frac{\text{fixed costs}}{\text{contribution per unit}}$$

$$= \frac{£4,500}{£4} = 1,125$$

If the burger van was able to achieve 3,000 sales, then the margin of safety would be:

3,000 – 1,125 = 1,875

Interpreting the data

Again, does this suggest that the firm should go ahead and sell at the festival? What other factors will need to be considered?

The margin of safety seems reasonable. The break-even level of output is relatively low in comparison to the projected sales. It also helps serve as a target for sales of the business over the 3 days. It can monitor how many sales it makes and use this to see where and when it has covered its costs. This is useful as the owners of the business will know, once they have achieved their break-even point, that every extra burger they sell is contributing £4 to profit.

You will probably face a number-crunching exercise which will involve manipulating the break-even formula in some way. You might be asked to calculate the break-even level of sales, or variations such as total contribution based on a certain level of sales. You might be asked to read off a break-even chart or recalculate a break-even point by changing the variable costs per unit, the selling price per unit or the fixed costs. This is known as 'what-if' analysis and is a great test of how well you understand and can manipulate the formula.

Budgeting

The definition of a budget is 'a forward financial plan'. In terms of calculations, you will be asked to look at variance analysis. A variance is as follows:

variance = the difference between an actual and a budgeted figure

→ Favourable variance results in profits being higher than forecast.
→ Adverse variance results in profits being lower than forecast.

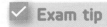

Exam tip

The key to budgeting is realising the difference between costs and revenues. If actual costs are lower than budgeted for, this will be in the business's favour — likewise, if actual revenues are higher than budgeted for. The exam questions are likely to investigate this and expect you to state whether the overall profit variance is favourable or adverse.

Worked example 2.10

Looking at the table below for two different festivals, comment upon the overall position of the business, its use of budgeting and its current performance. (Note that 'A' indicates an adverse variance while 'F' indicates a favourable variance.)

	Festival 1			Festival 2		
	Budget	Actual	Variance	Budget	Actual	Variance
Fixed costs	4,500	5,000	500 A	5,000	4,000	1,000 F
Variable costs	2,000	1,500	500 F	1,800	2,500	700 A
Revenue	10,000	7,500	2,500 A	9,000	12,500	3,500 F
Profit	3,500	1,000	2,500 A	2,200	6,000	3,800 F

Interpreting the data

So how good is the firm at budgeting and how helpful is it as a tool?

From the above table, it can be seen that the company has tried to adjust its budget to take into consideration the relatively lower sales that it achieved in the first festival. However, the second festival went much better for the company and it performed much better. What is important to note is that overall the business was profitable in both festivals — even though it was below target for the first festival.

It is also worth noting that you can calculate the actual number of sales from both festivals. At the first it only sold 1,500 burgers compared to 2,500 at the second. As an A*/A student you should be picking up on data like these and spotting the correlation between the variable costs and revenue figures.

Investment appraisal

Investment appraisal calculations are one way in which data can be used for decision making. There are three different methods a business can use to assess the merits of different investments: payback period, average rate of return (ARR) and net present value (NPV). We will look at each method in turn. Example data are given in Table 2.2.

Table 2.2 Data for two investment options

	Option 1	Option 2
Capital outlay (£)	(80,000)	(100,000)
Net income year 1 (£)	20,000	20,000
Net income year 2 (£)	20,000	30,000
Net income year 3 (£)	20,000	30,000
Net income year 4 (£)	20,000	40,000
Net income year 5 (£)	20,000	40,000

Method 1: payback period

This is the amount of time it takes to recoup the cash outlay of the investment.

Worked example 2.11

The example in Table 2.2 shows that option 1 pays back after 4 years as the £80,000 is recovered after four £20,000 cash inflows. However, in option 2 the payback is somewhere between years 3 and 4. After year 3, only £80,000 has been paid back. By the end of year 4, £120,000 has been paid back. Therefore, the payback period will be 3 years plus whatever is still required divided by the amount received in that year. We use the following formula to find the number of months to add on to 3 years:

$$\frac{\text{amount required}}{\text{amount received}} \times 12$$

$$\frac{20,000}{40,000} \times 12 = 6 \text{ months}$$

i.e. 6 months of year 4. The overall payback period is therefore **3 years 6 months**.

Method 2: average rate of return (ARR)

This is a more meaningful and complex method of investment appraisal. It works out a percentage return for each investment and can then be used in comparison to other measures such as ROCE (return on capital employed).

There are four simple steps:

1. Work out the total return of the project.
2. Subtract the cost of the project — this gives the net return.
3. Divide by the number of years — this gives the net return per annum.
4. Divide the net return per annum by the cost of the project and multiply by 100 to get a percentage.

Worked example 2.12

Using the options in Table 2.2 on page 23, we can calculate the ARR as follows.

	Option 1	Option 2
Total return	= 100,000	= 160,000
Subtract initial cost	100,000 – 80,000	160,000 – 100,000
Net return	= 20,000	= 60,000
Divide by number of years	20,000/5	60,000/5
Net return p.a.	= 4,000	= 12,000
Divide by cost of project	4,000/80,000	12,000/100,000
ARR	= 5%	= 12%

Method 3: net present value (NPV)

This method of investment appraisal takes into consideration the current value of the project to see whether it is worthwhile.

The logic is as follows. £100 today is worth more than £100 in 1 year's time — for example, £100 today could be invested and then be worth £100 + interest in 1 year's time. £10,000 in 1 year's time would be worth more than £10,000 in 5 years' time as it could have been invested and earned interest in that time.

NPV tries to calculate the present value of all the money coming into a business. It does this by using something called a **discount factor** which is basically an interest rate in reverse. For example, £10,000 in 1 year's time (assuming an interest rate of 10%) is worth £9,100 now. In other words, £9,100 invested now at 10% interest would be equal to £10,000 in a year's time.

Discount factors can be calculated or looked up in tables. Table 2.3 shows some selected discount factors. The relevant discount factors are always given in the exam.

Table 2.3 Selected discount factors

	5%	10%	15%
Year 0	1.00	1.00	1.00
Year 1	0.95	0.91	0.87
Year 2	0.91	0.83	0.76
Year 3	0.86	0.75	0.66
Year 4	0.82	0.68	0.57
Year 5	0.78	0.62	0.50

Worked example 2.13

All you need to do in the exam is multiply the relevant cash flow by the relevant discount factor. For example, at 10% the cash flows for the above two options would be as follows.

	Option 1	Option 2
Cost	£80,000 × 1.00 = (80,000)	£100,000 × 1.00 = (100,000)
Year 1	£20,000 × 0.91 = 18,200	£20,000 × 0.91 = 18,200
Year 2	£20,000 × 0.83 = 16,600	£30,000 × 0.83 = 24,900
Year 3	£20,000 × 0.75 = 15,000	£30,000 × 0.75 = 22,500
Year 4	£20,000 × 0.68 = 13,600	£40,000 × 0.68 = 27,200
Year 5	£20,000 × 0.62 = 12,400	£40,000 × 0.62 = 24,800

Once the present values have been calculated, you simply add them up and subtract the initial cost to work out the overall net present value for each of the two options. Therefore:

→ Option 1: NPV = −4,200
→ Option 2: NPV = +17,600

Interpreting the data

So which of the two options should the business go with and why? What other non-financial factors might it need to consider?

Using investment appraisal techniques is a vital part of the course and will feature in your exams. You are expected to consider the importance of the data together with other more qualitative factors such as the degree of risk, the amount of money to be invested, the likely accuracy of the forecasted data and whether the projects are worth proceeding with. From the two options offered, option 2 is clearly the best option in all measures. However, it is more expensive than option 1 and the projected inflows are not as consistent as option 1.

Practical finance: cash-flow forecasting

Cash-flow forecasting is a vital part of the success of any business. The timing of cash flowing into and out of a business

Exam tip

The key to this topic is making accurate calculations and then linking them back to the business. It is essential that you compare the data with the wider context of the business and it is always worth making an evaluative point that the projected returns are based on estimates and therefore cannot be fully relied upon. However, the decision-making tool is a useful indicator as to the relative merits of the options presented.

is fundamental to the firm's future. If the money flowing out of the business is greater than the money coming in, then the business will have difficulties operating. While a business can be profitable in the long term, not having enough cash in the short term can affect the firm's viability. It is essential that any firm keeps a close watch on all its dealings and cash-flow forecasting is essential.

Cash flow is simply calculated using the following formula:

cash flow = cash in − cash out

At A-level you will also be expected to work out the cumulative effects of cash flow month by month and the overall cash balance of the business.

Activity

You might be expected to calculate missing data using a table like the one below. See if you can complete the table based on the information given.

	Jun	July	Aug	Sept	Oct	Nov
Cash at start	200	230		210	200	190
Cash in	80	70			80	100
Cash out	50		100	80		70
Net cash flow		10	(30)			
Cash at end	230			200	190	

There are certain ways that a business can improve its cash-flow position. One way is to reduce the amount of credit that it offers its customers or potentially offer discounts for cash payments. This means that the business will attract a greater proportion of cash coming in.

In addition to this, the firm may look to delay payments to suppliers. This means that its own money will stay within the business longer. To do this, the firm will seek longer payment terms with suppliers — perhaps extending the time within which it must pay from 28 days to 56 days. This means that the firm does not have to pay out to suppliers so frequently. This will improve the cash-flow position of the firm and allow it to avoid potential problems. It means that it will be able to sell the goods before payment is required.

Firms may arrange an overdraft to cope with short-term cash-flow problems, but if this can be avoided then it will be better for the firm. Keeping track of the money coming in will allow a firm to budget accordingly and help identify when it might need the extra finance available. The firm will also need to present this information to its bank in order to set up an overdraft or take out a loan if required.

! Common pitfall

A pet hate for examiners is when candidates refer to profit and cash flow within the same sentence and use the terms interchangeably. They are two distinct measures. Profit considers the long-term performance of a business and factors in both costs and revenues. Cash flow is a more short-term measure and is purely concerned with the flow of money into and out of the business at a particular point in time.

If a business is cash poor, then it may face difficulties in the future as suppliers might be less willing to supply to it and this can then have knock-on effects on its relationship with customers. Therefore, cash flow is vital.

Finance for investors 1

In this section and the next we will look at ratio analysis. You will be expected to calculate many ratios as part of your exam and it is highly likely that you will be presented with a selection of the financial documents for a firm. You will need to use certain ratios to comment on the overall performance of the business and its financial health. You will be expected to use data from the two main financial documents: balance sheets and income (profit and loss) statements.

This section looks at **balance sheets** and at ratios which relate to them: **liquidity ratios**, **financial efficiency ratios** and the **gearing ratio**. The following section, the second one on finance for investors, will look at income statements and profitability ratios.

Balance sheets

A balance sheet shows the net worth of a business at a set point in time by looking at what the business owns (assets) and what it owes (equity and liabilities). It will always balance as the assets it owns must be funded in some way — through either borrowing money or using retained profits or owner's savings.

Key terms are set out in Table 2.4.

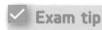

Exam tip

You will not be expected to construct a balance sheet from scratch. However, you need to be comfortable with the key parts of the balance sheet and the significance of the numbers. Has the firm's position improved or deteriorated? How can the business look to improve its financial health?

Table 2.4 Key terms relating to balance sheets

Term	Explanation
Inventories	the term for stocks
Total equity	the total amount of money pumped into a business from either retained profit or share capital
Non-current assets	fixed assets such as premises and vehicles which are likely to be kept for at least a year
Current assets	assets expected to vary in value on a daily basis, e.g. stock or cash; items that will be converted into cash within the next 12 months
Current liabilities	payments that need paying within a year, e.g. to creditors and suppliers; also known as 'payables'
Net current liabilities	current assets minus current liabilities
Non-current liabilities	debts that will take more than 1 year to pay, e.g. long-term bank loans
Debtor	someone who owes the business money, e.g. a customer
Creditor	someone the business owes money to, e.g. a supplier
Trade receivables	amounts owed by debtors
Trade payables	amounts owed by creditors

Table 2.5 shows a balance sheet for ABC Supermarket plc. We will be using the data for 2016 in the worked examples that follow, while the 2017 data are for later use in an activity.

Table 2.5 Balance sheet for ABC Supermarket plc

Balance sheet	2016 (£m)	2017 (£m)
Non-current assets (fixed assets)	3,000	2,500
Current assets:		
Inventories (stock)	250	230
Receivables (debtors)	150	140
Cash and other equivalents	180	190
Total current assets	**580**	**560**
Current liabilities	1,000	900
Net current liabilities	(420)	(340)
Non-current liabilities	(1,200)	(1,100)
Net assets	**1,380**	**1,060**
Total equity (shareholders' funds)	1,380	1,060

You will be expected to calculate various liquidity ratios and financial efficiency rations in relation to a balance sheet.

Liquidity ratios

Liquidity ratios look at the liquidity of the business, i.e. its ability to pay its debts and short-term bills. There are worked examples below for the **current ratio** and **acid test ratio**.

Worked example 2.14

ABC Supermarket plc, 2016

$$\text{current ratio} = \frac{\text{current assets}}{\text{current liabilities}}$$

$$= \frac{580}{1,000} = \mathbf{0.58:1}$$

Worked example 2.15

ABC Supermarket plc, 2016

$$\text{acid test ratio} = \frac{\text{current assets} - \text{stock}}{\text{current liabilities}}$$

$$= \frac{580 - 250}{1,000} = \mathbf{0.33:1}$$

Interpreting the data

Looking at the results above, should the firm be worried about its current performance? If so, why?

A current ratio of 0.58 means that the business has £0.58 of current assets for each £1 of current liabilities that it owes. This is worrying in isolation as the firm does not have enough current assets to cover what it owes. In general the following points hold:

→ A current ratio of between 2 and 3 is ideal.
→ A current ratio of less than 2 means that the business may have liquidity problems.
→ If the ratio is less than 1, this means that the business has fewer current assets than current liabilities, a very serious problem.
→ If the ratio is greater than 3, this is too high and means that the business has too much money in current assets that could be put to better use (i.e. there is an opportunity cost).

However, for a supermarket, the likelihood is that the firm purchases stock on credit and sells it before the firm is due to pay suppliers, so a current ratio of less than 1 is not uncommon.

The fact that the current ratio is below 1 is concerning as it makes the acid test ratio redundant — even if the firm sells all of its stock (unlikely), it cannot cover its current liabilities. Depending on the industry, you would still look to have a liquidity position that has an acid test ratio above 1.

Financial efficiency ratios

Financial efficiency ratios assess how efficiently management are controlling operations and the day-to-day running of the business. There are worked examples below for the following ratios: **inventory turnover**, **receivables days** and **payables days**. Note that information for these examples is to be found in both the balance sheet given in Table 2.5 (page 28) and the income statement given in Table 2.6 (page 32).

Worked example 2.16

ABC Supermarket plc, 2016

$$\text{inventory turnover} = \frac{\text{cost of sales}}{\text{inventory held}}$$

$$= \frac{£12,500m}{£250m} = 50$$

This ratio measures how many times a year a business sells and replaces its stock. A high inventory turnover figure means a business is frequently selling stock to generate sales revenue. For example, a figure of 50 means that the business sells its stock 50 times a year (approximately once a week).

This ratio can only be interpreted with some knowledge of the industry. For example, a bakery would have major problems if its inventory turnover was 12 whereas this might be quite a good figure for a car sales garage. A business such as a sandwich shop would expect an inventory turnover of 350 or more as it would be looking to sell its stock out almost every day of the year.

Worked example 2.17

ABC Supermarket plc, 2016

$$\text{receivables days} = \text{receivables} \times \frac{365}{\text{sales}}$$

$$= 150 \times \frac{365}{16,000} = \mathbf{3.42}$$

This simply measures how long it takes the company to collect debts owed by customers. For example, a figure of 3.42 means that it takes the business an average of 3.42 days to collect payments. This would be expected as nearly all sales from a supermarket are received at the point of sale.

Worked example 2.18

ABC Supermarket plc, 2016

$$\text{payables days} = \text{payables} \times \frac{365}{\text{cost of sales}}$$

$$= 1,000 \times \frac{365}{12,500} = \mathbf{29.2}$$

This measures how long it takes the business to pay its bills, for example how long it takes to pay suppliers. A figure of 29.2 means that it takes the business an average of 29.2 days to pay suppliers.

This figure compared to the receivables is very healthy. The business clearly offers very little credit to its customers and has a normal 28–30 days' credit with its suppliers. This suggests that the firm has a healthy cash-flow position, and while the current ratio is low, the firm is turning over its stock frequently and is in a strong financial position.

The gearing ratio

The gearing ratio focuses on the long-term financial stability of the business. Does it have too much debt? Can it afford the debt repayments? It shows how reliant the business is on borrowed money and this in turn indicates how it will cope if there are financial setbacks such as a recession or interest rate increases. Even when times are hard the banks will still expect their repayments.

 Exam tip

Gearing is a very commonly examined topic and examiners will expect you to suggest ways in which a firm can improve its gearing ratio. There are many options: a firm could look to repay loans, increase its overall profits or issue more shares to raise more equity. The difficulty with having a high gearing ratio is that the loan repayments can impact on the firm's cash-flow and liquidity position and might deter further investment into the business.

Worked example 2.19

ABC Supermarket plc, 2016

$$\text{gearing ratio} = \frac{\text{non-current liabilities}}{(\text{total equity} + \text{non-current liabilities})} \times 100$$

$$= \frac{1,200}{(1,380 + 1,200)} \times 100 = \mathbf{46.51\%}$$

The gearing ratio shows the percentage of a business's capital that has come from borrowing. A figure of 46.51% tells us that nearly half of the capital invested in the business is from loans.

A percentage of over 50% is a high gearing ratio. A business that is too highly geared will have to pay a lot of interest on its loans. In addition, it is very unlikely that banks will lend to companies with high gearing ratios, so it can become very difficult to raise extra finance.

A low gearing ratio carries an opportunity cost — the firm could be looking to borrow more finance to grow the business. However, the gearing ratio will be dependent on the objectives of the firm. Firms that look to grow organically will typically borrow less money from long-term external sources.

Activity

The ratios calculated in worked examples 2.14–2.19 above indicate the performance of ABC Supermarket plc for 2016. However, they need to be compared to how the firm has performed in other years, and they should also be compared to those for other firms within the industry.

- Having seen the worked examples for 2016, now see if you can calculate the same ratios for the company for 2017, using the figures provided in Table 2.5 (page 28) and Table 2.6 (page 32).

- Produce a table of each ratio against the 2016 figures to see if the company is performing better or worse than in the previous financial year.

- Next, research online for the current financial records of the major UK supermarkets (these are relatively easy to access). Use them to calculate up-to-date figures for the main ratios and compare their performance with that of ABC plc.

Finance for investors 2

In this section we will look at **income statements (profit and loss accounts)** and **profitability ratios**.

Income statements

Table 2.6 on page 32 shows an income statement for ABC Supermarket plc. We will be using the data for 2016 in the worked examples that follow, while the 2017 data are for later use in an activity.

Table 2.6 Income statement for ABC Supermarket plc

Income statement	2016 (£m)	2017 (£m)
Revenue (turnover)	16,000	18,000
Cost of sales	(12,500)	(13,500)
Gross profit	3,500	4,500
Expenses	(1,500)	(1,800)
Operating profit	2,000	2,700

Profitability ratios

Profitability ratios allow for the analysis of a firm's profits either in relation to its trading performance or in terms of the capital invested in that company.

Gross profit margin

This calculation looks at the profit before overhead costs have been taken away.

Worked example 2.20

ABC Supermarket plc, 2016

$$\text{gross profit margin} = \frac{\text{gross profit}}{\text{sales revenue}} \times 100$$

$$= \frac{£3,500m}{£16,000m} \times 100 = \textbf{21.88\%}$$

This ratio looks purely at trading and the higher the figure the better. Although a 21.88% margin sounds reasonable, the business has not deducted any overhead expenses. These overheads include rent, electricity, wages, rates and advertising.

Operating profit margin

This considers the actual profits after all expenses have been taken away.

Worked example 2.21

ABC Supermarket plc, 2016

$$\text{operating profit margin} = \frac{\text{operating profit}}{\text{sales revenue}} \times 100$$

$$= \frac{£2,000m}{£16,000m} \times 100 = \textbf{12.5\%}$$

The highest possible percentage is preferred here. The operating profit establishes whether the firm is efficient at controlling its expenses. If it has a falling operating profit margin, it means that expenses have increased and this will need to be investigated.

Return on capital employed

This allows potential investors to judge the return on their money and to make comparisons with alternative investments.

Worked example 2.22

ABC Supermarket plc, 2016

$$\text{return on capital employed} = \frac{\text{operating profit before tax}}{(\text{total equity} + \text{non-current liabilities})} \times 100$$

$$= \frac{£2,000}{(£1,380 + £1,200)} \times 100 = \textbf{77.5\%}$$

A return of 77.5% shows that, for £1 invested in the business, 77.5 pence operating profit is made.

The higher the figure the better — investors will compare this to other investment opportunities and decide if the risk/return is worth it. You should also realise the impact of changes in variables on the different ratios. For example, it is not a problem if a reduction in the gross profit margin has been caused by a reduction in the selling price if this leads to additional sales and an increase in the actual net profit.

Interpreting the data

Based on the income statement for the business, how is it performing overall? Are any other data or information required?

Overall ABC Supermarket plc is in a decent financial position. It is enjoying consistent profits and the margins are in line with the industry. Supermarkets tend to have slightly lower margins but on a high volume of sales.

What we have not done in the worked examples is calculate the figures for 2017. Whenever you use ratio analysis, it is always crucial that you compare the current performance with how the firm has performed previously and then compare this with the performance of other firms in the industry.

Activity

- Worked examples 2.20–2.22 were based on the 2016 figures for ABC Supermarket plc. Having seen these examples, now see if you can calculate the same ratios for the company for 2017, using the figures provided in Table 2.5 (page 28) and Table 2.6 (page 32).
- Produce a table of each ratio against the 2016 figures to see if the company is performing better or worse than in the previous financial year.
- Once you have completed the steps above, research online for the current financial records of the major UK supermarkets and compare their performance with ABC plc.

Production calculations

A final very useful set of calculations is to do with productivity. The results of these can offer excellent insight in terms of analysing the current state of the business. The formulae are given in Table 2.7.

Table 2.7 Formulae for production calculations

$\text{capacity utilisation}\% = \dfrac{\text{actual output in a given time period}}{\text{maximum possible output in a given time period}} \times 100$	
$\text{labour productivity} = \dfrac{\text{output per time period}}{\text{number of employees}}$	
$\text{uint costs (average costs)} = \dfrac{\text{total costs of production}}{\text{number of units of output produced}}$	
$\dfrac{\text{added value}}{\text{value added}} = \text{sales revenue} - \text{costs of bought-in goods and services}$	

Worked example 2.23

A pizza restaurant has a maximum capacity of 120 seats and expects to have 2 sittings per evening. The average number of pizzas it serves per evening is 160. It has 8 staff and each pizza is sold for £10. The total costs per evening are £600 which includes all its fixed and variable costs.

$$\text{capacity utilisation} = \frac{160}{240} \times 100 = \textbf{66.67\%}$$

$$\text{labour productivity} = \frac{160}{8} = \textbf{20 pizzas per employee}$$

$$\text{average unit costs} = \frac{£600}{160} = \textbf{£3.75}$$

$$\text{value added (per customer)} = £10 - £3.75 = \textbf{£6.25}$$

Interpreting the data

The eating-out sector has been troubled in recent times with major firms such as Jamie's Italian and Prezzo cutting back on their operations. Within this context and based on the data provided, how happy should this firm be with its performance?

Overall the pizza restaurant is performing nicely. It is unlikely that any restaurant business would be always operating at 100% capacity. Restaurants tend to be busier at weekends and quieter during the week. Therefore, firms will offer special deals midweek to try and increase capacity utilisation and generate more sales. Each pizza enjoys a decent mark-up and while customers could make pizzas at home, they are willing to pay a higher price for the value added by having someone make the pizza for them and enjoying the atmosphere of dining out.

You should know

> **The key formulae that you need to know are those for:**
> > marketing maths (market share, growth, size) and elasticity calculations
>
> > break-even and cost calculations
>
> > budgeting
>
> > investment appraisal
>
> > cash-flow analysis
>
> > ratio analysis
>
> > production calculations

> **All these calculations must be considered in the context of the firm and the industry in which it operates.**

> **Financial calculations are important but only reveal certain information — you will need to consider non-financial information as well.**

3 Reading skills

Learning outcomes

> To understand what to read and how to read effectively
> To understand the different types of reading, and when it is most appropriate to use each one
> To develop the skill of active reading
> To develop your own style of effective note taking
> To develop your own bank of relevant and useful case studies to use for particular theories

It is very easy to complete only the work you have been set for homework. However, as an A-level student, you should be looking to go beyond what is set and this is where the skills of reading come in.

Reading skills are neglected by many A-level business students. In the modern economy, much of the news that we receive comes from digital formats and it is rare for students to actively engage with extended text. This presents both a huge threat and also an enormous opportunity for you as an individual aiming for an A/A* grade. While there is talk of a change in the way subjects are examined, this is in reality a very long way off — the traditional exam paper that contains quite substantial amounts of text and data is here to stay for a considerable time.

Exams are by their nature time constrained and so it is essential to have the skills that allow you to process and access the key points from a particular piece of text. This will help you produce a response that directly answers the question set, bringing together the key parts of the case study.

The biggest single thing that will help you develop your writing skills is reading. Few students read enough, and so by simply reading this book and acting on the advice that follows, you will gain an advantage over the other 30,000 students you are competing against to get an A/A* grade.

What to read
Your class notes

The first thing you should be doing on a regular basis is reviewing and reading the notes you took in class. This will help you to remember what you were taught and help reinforce your understanding. Building in 30 minutes each day to revisit the topics covered will prove invaluable as you will find it much easier to recall particular topics and identify specific areas that you might be struggling with.

Textbook chapters

More schools and colleges are making use of the concept of flip learning. In this approach, instead of covering new topics in class, you arrive with the background reading completed before the topic is formally introduced. Even if your teachers do not utilise this technique, it is a very worthwhile and fulfilling exercise.

The modern textbooks have been written by very experienced examiners and teachers and are tailored specifically to the requirements of your individual exam board. By reading ahead, you can identify points that you might not fully understand and you can then seek out greater clarification from your teachers in class.

Wider reading

Wider reading is an expected part of any A-level study, and essential in a subject as fast-moving and ever-changing as business. To achieve the top grades, do not expect to be set specific reading by your teacher — instead go and look for topics and case studies that are of interest to you.

However, you must be aware of what makes something worth reading. It is important to keep up with the news, but you will not have time to read all of the business news articles every day. Instead, skim-read the business section and dip into the ones that are of interest to you. At the same time, you should have an awareness of the major stories, for example a high-street retailer shutting down and the reasons behind this. It would be useful to classify your articles into the ten key areas identified on page 11 of this guide.

Sources you could use include:
→ the business sections of Sunday newspapers
→ *Business Review* (a magazine written for A-level students)
→ *Bloomberg Businessweek*
→ *Harvard Business Review*
→ *Forbes*

You should also look for relevant books. Any decent bookshop will have a section devoted to business. While books on how to start up and run your own business are useful for practical applications, more highly recommended are books about individual entrepreneurs, describing how they started and what made them successful. All of these will contain insights that you can use to link the theory you are learning in class to the real world. They will also help you to build up a range of relevant examples and cases that you can then utilise within your essay responses.

Alternatives to reading

It is possible that you find reading difficult and challenging. The good news is that there are alternatives that can be equally useful as a source of information and in helping you to utilise examples and case studies in your arguments.

 Exam tip

Regardless of your exam board, it is vital to develop the skill of application and ensure you can bring in relevant examples for particular questions. You will be given case studies in the exams and these will be based on real businesses. Think of the advantage you will gain if you have already read up on some of these. While you can never fully predict what case studies will come up, they are likely to be drawn from news sources.

! Common pitfall

Once you begin to read more widely, there is a danger that you will end up telling stories in your responses rather than answering specifically the questions set. In that case the examiner, while perhaps entertained by your responses, will struggle to award you marks. The idea of reading is to enable you to compare and contrast effectively as well as showing good application and an appreciation that different businesses in different industries will be faced with different challenges.

Podcasts are an excellent source of up-to-date news and can easily be downloaded on to your devices. They can help you further your background understanding of the subject. The BBC is a good place to start as it offers excellent material which is free to download:

- *The Bottom Line* is a 30-minute programme that brings together three distinguished business people from a range of industries to discuss a particular topic and how it impacts on their particular business.
- *Peter Day's World of Business* is similarly organised into a range of topics and previous shows can be downloaded.
- *BBC Business Daily* has up-to-date and relevant examples of what is happening in the business world.
- *Wake Up to Money* is similar to the above, and goes on air at 5 a.m. each day. It has some very accessible content that will keep you up to date with the major current news stories impacting on businesses both large and small.

In addition, YouTube is your friend — there are a host of business-related videos that can assist you. TED talks on business are often relevant, interesting and inspirational. Forbes.com also has a host of excellent videos (albeit with a slight American bias). For revision purposes, a new channel that is gaining in popularity is *Taking the Biz* — this channel enables you to search and review key topics that you might be struggling with.

Reading techniques

There are three main reading techniques that you should aim to adopt in your reading around the subject — skimming, scanning and active reading. These are all important skills that will help you develop your understanding of the key theories.

Before reading you should ensure that you know what you are trying to achieve. For example, are you reading a magazine article to find out about a particular business mentioned in class or are you just reading your textbook to gain further knowledge on a topic you have struggled with? Knowing before you begin is important, as otherwise you will end up spending a lot of time reading without gaining very much from it.

Skim reading

When you skim read, you are looking to gain an understanding of what the general theme of the text is, so that you can decide whether reading it will actually help you to achieve your goal.

Skim reading involves:

→ looking for key headings and identifying key words

→ reading the opening paragraph

→ looking at pictures, charts, graphs or other data and gleaning how useful or relevant this information is

Skim reading should give you a clear idea of what the whole article, chapter or book is about, from which you can decide if further reading is needed or if the piece is not useful.

> **! Common pitfall**
>
> Avoid using skim reading as your only form of reading. The use of digital devices often means that you only pick up a little piece of a story. The aim of skim reading is to help you identify a piece of reading that will help you delve into a subject deeper.

Scan reading

Scan reading is useful if you are looking for specific information or evidence for an essay you are writing. It also forms a key part of your exam technique. When you are given a case study within the exam itself, the overall timing of the exam will build in time to read and highlight the key issues in the case study. However, as you tackle different questions, you will need to be able to scan through the case study and pick up valuable nuggets of information that you can then utilise in your answers. The starting point must be to identify exactly what you are looking for before you begin.

In terms of looking for key figures, these are usually found in the appendices of data, but on occasion they can also be found in the body of text. For example, when calculating a break-even output, you might be given cost data in an appendix, but projected sales in the case study. Therefore, you need to be able to quickly scan to the appropriate parts of the text to glean the information that you require.

Active reading

Whereas with scan reading you are aiming to identify the key facts and data, the aim of active reading is to make sure that you fully understand the terminology and concepts in the text, but also think about the wider context and how the content links to what you have previously studied. For active reading to be most effective, you should be using it to develop more detailed notes. It is highly recommended that you engage with this guide in the form of active reading.

You should include the following in your notes:

→ **Definitions**. These should be full and precise. You could build up a definition/glossary section in your files or alternatively have a definitions section for each topic.

→ **Explanations**. Include concise explanations of any complex concepts. You should be able to write a short paragraph that covers the topic.

→ **Links.** What other areas of the specification could the topic be linked to?

→ **Examples.** Try to think of three relevant examples from a variety of industries that help support the concept.

One of the most important tips that you should heed is to build up a series of case studies that you can utilise when answering some of the longer, more open-ended essay questions you are likely to face in your exams. Key areas/industries that you could focus on are highlighted on page 11 of this guide.

Many of the articles in the business sections of newspapers, magazines and websites only need to be scan-read to get the main points. However, having scan-read one, you might decide there is plenty of useful information that could form an excellent case study. As you read through the material, try to identify the key topics mentioned and consider how you could use the case study to build up a chain of argument in a response. Keep the case study in a section of your folder along with other articles.

> **! Common pitfall**
>
> Under the pressure of the exam, the temptation is to highlight and underline every key point and fact and figure. This undermines the effectiveness of your reading and makes it hard to go back to the really important points that need to be drawn from the text. Be selective in what you pick out. The most important highlighting or underlining you can do is on the trigger words of the question as this will help you structure your answer precisely to fit the question set. This will be covered in more detail in Chapters 4 and 5.

> **✓ Exam tip**
>
> When reading a case study, ask yourself the following three questions:
> - What are the key characteristics of the business?
> - What is the nature of the industry that the business operates in?
> - What key issues/challenges is the business facing right now?
>
> Answering these questions will help you to apply your answer more effectively. By considering the all-important wider context, you will be able to extend your responses more analytically.

Using an article for a case study

In this section we illustrate how you can use an article for a case study. Our example article provides suitable material for a case study of the situation of the UK restaurant industry in early 2018.

Identifying key points

The sample article is provided in the annotated example below. The annotations show how you could pick out key points from the article, which you could then write up in note form.

Annotated example 3.1

Trouble in the kitchen

Many of the well-known restaurant chains on the UK high street have announced closures. The burger chain Byron is to close up to 20 restaurants after agreeing a rescue plan with lenders and landlords. The Jamie Oliver Restaurant Group announced that it would shut down 12 of its 37 Jamie's Italian restaurants, in the second round of closures to take place within a year. The Restaurant Group, owner of Frankie & Benny's and Garfunkel's, has seen its shares lose two thirds of their value since the start of 2015.

Clearly the situation facing a number of chains is not unique and represents a challenge for them all. The key issue is *why* are they struggling?

There is currently pressure on the entire UK food sector, with businesses required to pay the new living wage and the apprenticeship levy, and also being faced with upwards-only rent reviews. All this means that costs are rising significantly. At the same time, consumer confidence is still relatively weak and there is a lot of choice available for customers, who are very sensitive to pricing and simply not eating out as often. A further factor is an increase in food and ingredients costs, especially with the relatively weak pound since Britain's vote to leave the European Union, which has led to importing items becoming relatively more expensive.

Causes are identified here, suggesting a combination of rising costs, too much choice and other external factors.

There are arguably also just too many restaurants. With so much choice, there is little customer loyalty — and greater use of social media has increased customer awareness of a wider range of available eating choices. Casual dining firms have found consumers reluctant to spend, and chains have been forced to discount in order to gain customers, so that profit margins are squeezed even tighter.

> Confirms points identified previously, expanding on the issue of choice and stressing an over-saturated market, but adds in discounting of prices and narrower profit margins.

At the same time restaurants are under pressure to keep up with current trends in consumer technology. Younger customers want to record their own activities and to be seen in a 'cool' environment, so restaurants need to be 'Instagrammable' to attract them. However, investment is needed to create a suitable environment, and that is a challenge, particularly when the industry is struggling. In addition, restaurants need to be aware of the change in consumer tastes with higher demand for healthy eating and sustainable food sourcing. Firms need to adapt, but don't necessarily have the funds to do so.

> Discusses the pressures from changing patterns in consumer technology and lifestyle preferences, and the difficulties in reacting to these changes due to financial constraints.

The firms are also being impacted by the rise of food delivery firms such as Just Eat and Deliveroo. On the one hand, they can increase sales, and they increase profit on balance. On the other hand, they can lead to difficulties if there are insufficient staff to both deal with takeaway orders and attend to the needs of customers in the restaurant. There are also other disadvantages: the high commission charged for delivery by the food delivery firms, and the lost opportunities to sell profitable extras such as drinks within the restaurants.

> Discusses the changing nature of the market with the rise of delivery over eat-in: a social change.

Developing an argument

A number of fundamental concepts are mentioned in the article. Many of them are external factors that fall under the categories used in PESTEL analysis (political, economic, social, technological, environmental and legal).

The key external issues raised are the changes in economic, social and technological areas. How can these be used in developing a line of argument? Annotated example 3.2 provides an illustration.

Annotated example 3.2

Below is a sample essay title (to which we will return in Chapter 5, when we look in detail at essay writing).

To what extent are the demand on and costs of a business mainly determined by factors outside of its control?

The article above could be used to develop arguments that support this view. An example is given in the paragraph below which could form part of a response to the question.

> Restaurant chains such as Byron are clear examples of businesses that have been impacted by external factors. With a downturn in the economy, customers have lower disposable income in the main, which means that they are likely to eat out less, and that when they do they are likely to be more price sensitive and to choose the best-value option. It is also likely to mean that the restaurants will see fewer consumers eating in and more opting for a takeaway, which will impact on their sales of extra drinks and also add to their costs as they need to pay for delivery drivers' wages. At the same time, these firms are facing rising costs — with the pound being weak, imports of raw materials (ingredients) are relatively more expensive, which cuts into their overall profit margins. This means that the firms have less finance available to react to the changing demands in the restaurant sector and cannot react as quickly.

This paragraph takes several points mentioned in the article and uses them to build up a good chain of reasoning that is relevant to the question posed. It identifies each point and then develops it in context and shows analysis.

You should know

> Read over your notes after class.
> Organise your files — successful students are frequently the most organised.
> Read a textbook before or after a topic has been covered to help your understanding.
> Keep abreast of what is happening in the business world from either digital or paper-based sources.
> Identify useful articles, make notes from them and build up a section for these in your files.
> Useful information can come from a number of sources.
> Make sure that you edit and organise your notes before you start revising, so that they do not become too cumbersome.

4 Writing a short response

The exam questions will include both short-answer questions that are testing only the first three assessment objectives (i.e. knowledge, application and analysis) and questions needing longer, more extended answers which will focus on all of the assessment objectives. In this chapter, we will focus on the short-answer questions. However, it is important to note that the approach used for these responses can then be carried forward to the longer-answer questions simply with the addition of AO4 (evaluation). If you can master the techniques put forward in this chapter, then it will also help you with the longer-answer questions.

Regardless of your exam board, you will face some short-answer questions which test your ability to recall certain factual aspects of the specification. The aims of the A-level exams include testing how well you know key parts of the syllabus and what you have learnt. One of the new mantras is 'knowledge is the gatekeeper' and therefore it is vital that you can demonstrate your ability to answer precisely the question set and clearly show your awareness of the particular theories being examined.

It is important to know how your exam board is going to assess you for each type of question. Information on the mark breakdowns for each exam board and the styles of question they use can be found in the 'Exam board focus' section at the end of this guide. In this chapter we will begin by looking at the different command words that exam boards use and what skills they are aiming to test.

Command words

In order to maximise your potential, it is essential that you become very comfortable with the different command words that are used by the exam boards. These are common across the boards and are used specifically to enable you as the candidate

> ! **Common pitfall**
>
> Avoid spending too much time on short-answer questions. These are not worth many marks in the grand scheme of things and you need to stick to timing so that you can focus on the questions that are worth more marks.

> ! **Common pitfall**
>
> It is a mistake to think that short-answer questions simply require regurgitation of knowledge. They provide an opportunity to demonstrate what you know, but this must be developed and relevant, not simply a list.

to understand exactly what the question is requiring from you. A command word is the word or phrase that tells you exactly what your response should do.

Table 4.1 shows some typical command words with their meanings.

Table 4.1 Typical command words and what they mean

Command word	Meaning
Analyse	Build up a chain of reasoning, using connectives (see page 46) and explaining how different aspects of the theory relate to each other
Assess	In what ways can the concept be challenged — what are the main advantages and disadvantages of the suggested issue?
Compare	What are the similarities and differences between the arguments?
Describe	What are the main features (what it looks like) and the main issues arising from the piece of theory?
Examine	What are the key terms and knowledge relevant to the concept? What is the relative importance of each concept?
Explain	What is the concept and how or why is it important?

As mentioned earlier, short-answer questions tend to focus on AO1 (knowledge), along with AO2 (application) and AO3 (analysis). The skill of analysis is crucial — not just for the shorter responses, but also for the more extended writing that we will discuss in the next chapter. It is arguably one of the most challenging skills and it is certainly one you must aim to master if you want to be successful.

You may wonder whether you should start a short response with a definition. The answer is yes, wherever this would be appropriate. While full marks *can* be awarded without a definition, it is a good policy to include one. If you go off topic and fail to correctly interpret the question asked, you are in danger of being awarded zero marks for your response. Starting with a definition gives you the opportunity to pick up content marks, even if you later go astray.

Also, keep in mind the new mantra of 'knowledge is the gatekeeper' mentioned earlier — a definition highlights to the examiners that your subject knowledge is sound and gets them 'on side' early. Therefore, going forward, *always* consider starting a short or longer answer with a definition.

Deconstructing the question

Most short-answer questions will share a common structure. Identifying the parts of the question before you start to write is important. Make sure you look at the precise wording of the question and keep an eye out for words that have been pluralised. An annotated example is given on page 45.

Exam tip

You need to show you can develop a sustained chain of reasoning, building up an argument step by step — but avoid simply reproducing a generic series of points that could apply to any business. Your arguments must be relevant to the question set and use the key hooks in the question. Examiners will not be impressed by rote-learned generic responses, so make sure you apply your answer directly to the scenario presented.

Exam tip

Make sure you have a coloured pen or highlighter in the exam. At the very least you should aim to underline the key command words, topic and focus in a question before you begin. Before you start writing you need to understand exactly what the question is asking from you.

Annotated example 4.1

This example illustrates how to deconstruct a question. Consider the following:

Analyse the consequences of a firm looking to use debt factoring to improve its cash-flow position.

The parts of this question can be identified as follows:

→ Analyse is the command word.

→ Debt factoring in relation to improving cash flow is the key topic.

→ Consequences suggests that you should put forward at least two arguments. Remember that consequences can be both positive and negative.

Note the following concerning **application** here. It would be typical for the above question to be based on a set of data that you would be expected to use in order to apply the theory to the case study. It would be likely to give information about the current cash-flow position of the firm. There should therefore be a focus on the relative importance of making use of debt factoring in relation to the actual situation.

On a question such as this, you should aim to produce two detailed and chunky paragraphs giving a series of connected points that each build on the previous point. It would also be advisable to show that you understand the concept of debt factoring as this will earn you knowledge marks and help you to access the key aspects of the question.

Business exams are based primarily on the mark-a-minute principle. Factoring in reading time, you should not be spending any longer than 10 minutes on a question such as this. The way to ensure that you have your timing right is to practise. There is no point in spending 30 minutes writing a response for homework, when in the exam itself you will only have 10 minutes — get used to writing responses under timed conditions.

Remember that you do not need to be writing non-stop during the whole 2 hours of the exam. Time spent planning is normally time very well spent. You can achieve the maximum marks on the question above by writing two very focused and clear paragraphs. That will work much better than 'waffling on'.

Writing your response

Building an argument

As you set out to write your response, you need to remember how the marks are awarded. So how do you demonstrate knowledge, application and analysis?

→ Don't assume that the examiner knows what you mean. It might seem obvious from your point of view but examiners can't read your mind. It is worth trying to write a response that treats the examiner as someone who has never studied business before.

→ Every time you make a point, aim to explain it as if you are teaching someone about an area that they have never covered before. Far too many students make points that are relevant, but fail to explain them. They assume that the examiners can follow the logic, but never develop their points to build a sequential chain of argument following a step-by-step approach.

> **! Common pitfall**
>
> Be mindful of whether you need to give both sides of the argument. On the shorter essay questions, the focus is often on just one side of the argument. For example, you might be asked to analyse the benefits of primary market research. Too often, students think they should give the counter-arguments — but this is not answering the question and will not pick up marks as it is not relevant.

→ Analysis is about forging a series of links that enable the examiner to follow the logic in your arguments. They are looking for a series or chain of developed points that are relevant to the business in the case study. You do not want the examiner to be thinking 'why?' or asking themselves 'and then what?'. Far too many students make a lot of simple points without taking them to the next level.

Think of building an argument as blowing up a balloon. To get the balloon inflated you need a sustained number of puffs to make it work. Each time you make a point, think how it can be developed further.

Try not to be too assertive and definitive in your responses. Things in business are very rarely definite, so you need to be using phrases like the following:

→ 'This could lead to...'

→ '...which may then result in...'

→ '...which has the potential to then lead to...'

→ '...which could then cause...'

These are known as **connectives** and help you to build a sustained argument by showing the connections between a series of points. This is not easy to do in practice. You really need to train yourself to become analytical. In practice responses, after every sentence try and think how the next sentence can inflate the balloon (your argument) even further.

The following annotated example shows how an effective chain of argument can be built up.

Annotated example 4.2

Analyse the consequences of a firm looking to use debt factoring to improve its cash-flow position.

Clear, precise and accurate definition.

Nice, effective chain of argument.

The use of debt factoring involves selling off your short-term debts to an outside organisation that will take on the responsibility for chasing up the debt owed. It normally provides a business with 90% of the monies owed and then looks to recover the full amount owed to the business. The consequence of this is that the debt factoring will give the business an immediate source of cash, which can then be used to deal with the payables due and thus gives the firm a significant boost of cash, which will improve its short-term cash-flow position. Cash flow is about the timing of money coming into the business (receivables) against money leaving the business (payables). This will help the firm's liquidity and help the firm in terms of its credit rating and reduce the chances of having long-term debts and money issues, which will mean that the business can access future sources of finance more easily.

Linking back to the question, i.e. impact on cash-flow position.

However, a negative consequence of this is that the debt factoring company will take a percentage of the money, and so the firm does not receive the full amount owed. The firm will have to consider the seriousness of its current cash-flow position as to whether meeting the need for some immediate injection of funds is preferable to receiving the full amount. This involves an opportunity cost financially, but the time, effort and stress saved in chasing up the debt might offset this.

Looking at a possible negative consequence — could be developed a little more but overall an effective response.

Overall comments: The response starts with a definition of debt factoring and shows good understanding of the concept. It then links this to cash flow. The response also builds a chain of argument. It explains how debt factoring can have a positive impact on cash flow and develops this point nicely. The second point is developed less fully, but still demonstrates that the concept is understood and an argument is being put forward.

The PEAL approach

There are a number of techniques that you can utilise to make your response effective and analytical. One such technique is the PEAL approach:

→ P = Point
→ E = Explanation and example
→ A = Analysis and application to the case study
→ L = Linked back to the actual question set

Point

You should identify the 'point' of your paragraph in your opening sentence. The point could be simply demonstrating that you have understood the key term in the question. However, it probably should be more about showing that you know what the question is asking and what your arguments are going to be about.

Explanation and example

With the point made, or the key term defined, you then must explain what it means. You are looking to explain 'how' and 'why' the point is relevant and then use relevant examples that help explain your point. Examples are important as they not only support your point, but also show that your theory has some relevance in reality or is making use of the data from the case study.

However, you should be wary of becoming descriptive or drifting into a story. You should aim to make specific mention of the business or the data, which will help your argument come alive.

Analysis and application to case study

With the point made and explanation given, you then need to be stretching the line of analysis and argument to make a series of sequential points. These must not be generic — they should make use of the business in question and the data given.

Linked back to question

Once you have developed your line of argument, ask yourself whether it is still focused on the actual question asked. Could you work out the question from just reading the response? If you could, then it probably demonstrates that you have specifically answered the question. After every point and paragraph that you write, re-read the question to check that you are still focused fully on its precise wording.

Examples to compare

Annotated examples are given below for two different short-answer questions. For each question, two different responses are shown for you to compare. This should help you to see how strong responses are constructed and how weaker responses go astray.

Annotated example 4.3

Analyse the benefits to the retailer John Lewis of offering good customer service.

Response 1

Offering good customer service is a way of differentiating your product and business from rivals. It is also relatively easy to establish through training of staff and this helps build a culture within the organisation as well as improving the reputation of the business. John Lewis and Waitrose recruit their staff for their personality and willingness to help. This then means that customers are more likely to approach them and recommend the business to

A clear benefit identified.

other people — helping the business increase its customer base as well as encouraging repeat business from its existing customers who are impressed by the level of care and attention they receive.

Benefit developed and explanation given of how it works within the context of the business.

While training staff can be expensive initially, the long-term benefits are likely to outweigh the cost as staff are likely to be more motivated and happy in their work, as customers appreciate the care and attention they provide, which makes staff less likely to leave. This will reduce the labour turnover figures for John Lewis, which will in turn lower the need to recruit and train new staff. It also helps the business when it does need to recruit as people will want to work for a company that is friendly and provides excellent service to its customers. The monitoring of customer service is also relatively easy to carry out using mystery shoppers or by internal appraisal of staff. Overall, offering good customer service will be a way of providing something different that makes the business stand out and will lead to a relatively cheap way of promoting the company and differentiating it from other retailers.

A really well-developed chain of reasoning using connectives and a sequence of connected points.

Drifting slightly from the actual wording of the question and into 'how' to monitor customer service. This material is actually 'NAQ' (examiner code for 'not answering the question').

Final sentence brings the response back to the actual question.

Overall comments: The response starts with a clear point (P) and this is then explained (E) in relation to the business in the question. An example (E) of exactly how customer service would benefit the specific business would have been useful. However, the example given is then developed into an analytical (A) argument.

The second paragraph feels a little generic and is perhaps not always precisely about customer service, but the way it is written covers this and it delivers a superb chain of argument about how the firm benefits from the focus on customer service with loyal and motivated workers. The penultimate sentence drifts away from the question somewhat, before the final sentence clearly brings the argument back to the focus of the question. Overall, a good response.

Response 2

Customer service is about making sure you treat your customers with respect and kindness. It could help John Lewis as it means that customers return each week and are loyal to the company. It could also help the workers at John Lewis feel motivated and happy. The company would however have to spend substantial time and money training its workers in how to offer good customer service and this will be expensive and time-consuming, which will cut into its profits and mean that it suffers financially. It could also be necessary to offer customer service to give the business a USP over its rivals, which will allow the company to gain market share and this could lead to long-term benefits for the company.

Definition a bit imprecise.

Point made but not explained.

Why? Not explained again.

Student is not answering the question — focus should be on the benefits of good customer service.

All rather generic and not really fully developed.

Overall comments: The response is muddled and fails to pick out exactly what the question requires. The definition lacks precision and points are made but not developed. The student then drifts away from the actual question and into the drawbacks of maintaining good customer service. The response fails to build up a sustained chain of reasoning.

Annotated example 4.4

Analyse the benefits for Nissan of having a well-motivated workforce.

Response 1

Having a well-motivated workforce will have significant benefits for Nissan. If workers are happy in their work and enjoy their job, they are less likely to leave, which will not only reduce labour turnover, but also the need to recruit and train new workers. This will have a substantial cost saving for the firm. It will also mean that workers' productivity will increase as they are

Making a point but not actually doing anything with it. Just a statement at this stage.

likely to be happier in their roles and buy into the company's mission and objectives, which means that they are more likely to adapt to new working practices and less likely to resist change. In the context of a technological industry this can prove very valuable as they are likely to be more able to learn and develop new skills.

Feels a little generic to begin with, but then the response builds and develops an interesting line of argument that recognises the context of the industry and the need to move with the times.

A second benefit is that, if workers are motivated and enjoy what they are doing, they are likely to become increasingly efficient and skilled in their particular roles and will become specialised in their chosen role. This is likely to lead to a greater quality of the product/service being produced and an increased reputation for Nissan which will mean that it can potentially increase its market share. Nissan has gained a reputation for the build quality of its vehicles and this is down to having such a productive and motivated workforce, which means that Nissan can increase its competitiveness within the industry.

A second point that applies the argument specifically to the business and how this can have substantial benefits for the firm.

Overall comments: The response starts with a point (P) that is more of a statement than an explanation. However, the point is then explained (E) with a line of argument about the benefits that motivated workers will bring to the firm specifically. This is applied directly to the business and links different aspects of the business curriculum to the topic, such as mission and overcoming difficulties with change.

The second paragraph is arguably even stronger as it really analyses why motivated workers will benefit Nissan specifically and explains this very well. Overall, this is an excellent response. It is clearly focused on the question throughout and focuses fully on the business.

Response 2

Nissan is well known for having a well-motivated workforce and it has worked hard on ensuring that this is the case with careful selection of workers and setting up in areas of relatively high unemployment as this gives it access to a wider pool of skilled labour. This means that it is likely to face lower labour turnover, and to have the prospect of more productive workers because workers do not have the opportunity to move to a rival firm as they do not have as many options as in other areas with higher employment.

This is a decent line of argument but unfortunately not relevant to the actual question asked.

Being well motivated means that the workers do not need to be monitored as much because they can be trusted to get on with their roles with less supervision and control. This means that the firm could potentially employ fewer managers and within Nissan they employ single status — meaning that all workers are treated equally and therefore there is a lack of hierarchy within the organisation and workers will feel more valued.

This is a reasonable point and could be valid. However, it is not backed up and instead the candidate chooses to discuss the issue of single status, which again is of little relevance.

Overall comments: This is a classic example of a strong response but not to the question that is set. The student clearly knows some background information on Nissan but this does not lead to effective application as it is not being used to answer the question directly. The argument about high unemployment is developed reasonably, but is not being linked to the question about the benefits of having a well-motivated workforce.

Likewise the second line of argument is rather tenuous and assertive. The student has failed to identify relevant points in the context of the question and overall it feels as though they are writing about some facts they have learnt about Nissan.

The shorter analysis-mark questions are not easy. It really is a skill to build up your responses. However, it is a challenge worth persevering with. These questions account for an important part of the overall examination marks. In addition, the skills that you learn and embed on the lower-tariff questions come in equally useful for the longer-response questions as they require exactly the same kind of development of points. We will look at these longer-response questions in detail in the next chapter.

You should know

> 'Explain' and 'Analyse' questions test three skills: knowledge, application and analysis.
> Strong answers identify key arguments, explain them in context and link back to the question set.
> Strong answers include definitions which are full and precise.
> Strong answers analyse issues in chains of reasoning that are detailed, logical and built up step by step.

5 Writing a long essay

Learning outcomes

> To understand the meaning of command words that will be used in your exams
> To be able to deconstruct any exam question so that you will know exactly what it is asking
> To know how to plan a long-essay response
> To know how to structure a long-essay response
> To understand how to apply your response effectively to the question set and bring in relevant examples

Writing a response to the higher-mark essay questions is often the area that students fear the most and find most challenging. While it might appear as a threat, it can also be seen as a huge opportunity to showcase your skills and what you have learnt — it can make the single biggest difference to your chances of achieving an A*/A grade.

Remember that only the top 15% of students are generally awarded the highest grades. The longer-response questions account for the majority of the marks awarded across the papers (see the 'Exam board focus' section at the end of this guide for details), so it really should go without saying that you must aim to master these questions above all. However, developing your essay-writing technique is likely to take time and effort — the good news is that you are reading this guide, which will offer you key tips to be successful.

The difference between constructing a short analytical response (discussed in the previous chapter) and writing a longer essay comes down to just one word: evaluation. The skill of evaluation is arguably even more important than that of analysis and can prove just as difficult to master. Evaluation involves weighing up, then prioritising, and coming to a fully justified judgement about what a business should do in a particular situation. Students are often quite poor at evaluation, which is surprising as teenagers are normally very good at giving and justifying their opinions!

Command words

The command word is the word or phrase that tells you what to do. However, be aware that for longer essays, the command words can be less important than some of the small words included within the question. It is also vital to remember that, whichever command word is used, you are still expected to cover and focus on all of the first three assessment objectives (knowledge, application and analysis) before coming to an overall judgement.

Table 5.1 shows typical command words used for longer essays and explains what they mean.

Table 5.1 Typical command words for longer essays and their meanings

Command word	Meaning
Discuss	Usually, you are asked to 'discuss' a given statement. You are effectively writing a debate about the statement, analysing reasons why it could be considered reasonable or not, and making a reasoned judgement on these reasons.
Evaluate	Reach a judgement as to how far you agree or disagree with a given statement or view by analysing a range of factors on both sides of the argument and evaluating their significance and/or strength before reaching a well-justified conclusion.
To what extent	This kind of question is asking you to judge something on a sliding scale, from 'not at all' to 'completely' or somewhere in the middle. To achieve this you need to analyse and evaluate different viewpoints and make your own overall judgement as to where on the sliding scale you believe the truth to be.
Justify your view	Having discussed both sides of an argument, what is the most important issue and why? You must express your exact judgement and opinion very clearly.

Deconstructing the question

Most long-answer questions will share a common structure. Identifying the parts of the question before you start to write is important. Make sure you look at the precise wording of the question and identify the words that carry the most significance.

Too many students will skim-read the question and begin writing without even pausing. Remember that you are not being tested on what you know; you are being tested on your ability to use what you know to answer the specific question asked. It is crucial to understand that knowing 'stuff' is not enough for good marks at this level of study. You must be able to distinguish between answering the question set and simply writing everything that you know about a particular topic.

Identifying the hooks

While the command words help signpost what type of question is being asked, other aspects of the wording are also important. You also need to identify the key topics/issues in the question, and the key 'hooks' of the question. The hooks are different from command words and are arguably the most important parts to identify. What exactly are you being asked to do? What are the significant words and why are they so important? You should underline or highlight the hooks. See annotated example 5.1 for illustration.

The focus of each question is changed slightly by the use of different wording. Small words can carry significant influence and need to be seized upon. They will often guide you to structure your response in a particular way. Later in the chapter we will return to several of the questions in this example, to show how you could plan and write suitable responses to them.

 Exam tip

As the skill of evaluation is given considerable weighting, it is vital that you are able to make judgements that are justified. Examiner feedback shows that candidates often fail to do this. Certainly, analysis is important in building your response — putting together the key arguments and developing both the theory and how it is relevant to the business in the question. However, it is the evaluation skill that carries a significant proportion of the marks on the longer-answer questions. Evaluation is the final piece of the jigsaw and it is essential that you master this skill to achieve an A grade.

! Common pitfall

Students often have well-rehearsed essays that they are comfortable with and that they simply regurgitate when a similar question comes up in an exam. Avoid this! If you do not answer the exact question asked, you will not do well.

Annotated example 5.1

The example questions below are highlighted to show their distinct elements. The key to the colours used is given at the end of the box.

1. A business has recently started to use Elkington's Triple Bottom Line to assess its overall performance. To what extent do you think the business is likely to have higher profits as a result of this?

2. To what extent is the nature of the product the most important influence on the marketing mix of all businesses?

3. To what extent are the demand on and costs of a business mainly determined by factors outside of its control ?

4. A business wants to increase the productivity of its workforce. To what extent is the greater use of training likely to be an effective way for the business to achieve this?

5. Is the power of buyers or the likelihood of new entrants the bigger threat to ABC plc? Justify your view.

6. Most journalists blamed the fall in ABC plc's profits on either a failure to control costs or a slowdown in the growth of the global economy . Which of these two reasons do you think is the main cause ? Justify your view.

Command words	Key topics/issues	Hooks

However, before you even begin to write your response you need to make sure you have it planned out. It is important to strike the correct balance between planning and writing. Many students spend no time in planning, which is a recipe for disaster, while others spend too long and don't leave enough time to actually put together the response. Therefore the skill of planning is essential to master.

Planning your essay

The most important aspect of the plan is that it should help you to stay fully focused on the question throughout your response. This will give you confidence when you are writing up your answer: by sticking to the plan you will be sticking to the actual essay question and therefore giving the examiners exactly what they are looking for.

The starting point of the plan should actually be about the final answer. What is the decision you need to reach? From this you can work backwards. We will show how this works shortly, but before that we need to remember that a well-written long-essay answer is always organised with a clear structure that makes it easy to read. Remember as well that you need to be showcasing all of the lower-order skills of knowledge and application. However, as your answer builds, so too should you be bringing in the key lines of analysis and evaluation.

A suitable structure should contain the elements shown in Table 5.2.

Table 5.2 Elements of essay structure

Element	How to write it
Introduction	Define the key terms and the main focus of the question. Try to make clear what your final answer is and how you are going to get there.
Development	Explain the relevant theory and apply it to the context of the question.
Analysis	Identify the important issues and analyse in a logical step-by-step chain of argument.
Evaluation	Draw judgements from the analysis based on the arguments you have put forward.
Conclusion	Directly answer the question and pay careful attention to the command word and the key 'hooks'. Make it clear what *your* opinion is.

An alternative structure that can be used to help you with the development of your paragraphs is given by the PUCCER technique. In each paragraph, you should be aiming to include the following:

➜ **Point** — make it clear what you are arguing
➜ **Understanding** — explain your point, with examples if suitable
➜ **Causes**
➜ **Consequences**
➜ **Evaluation** — of the point you have made
➜ **Refer** — back to the question

The wording of the question and the total marks available will normally indicate the number of arguments/paragraphs you should aim to have. Remember that the first paragraph will normally include a short introduction and explanation of the key terms in the question and the final paragraph should make it very clear what the final judgement is.

As a very rough rule of thumb:

➜ 16 marks: aim for 3 to 4 paragraphs.
➜ 20–25 marks: aim for 4 to 5 paragraphs.

Steps in planning

There is a technique to planning your responses. Once you have highlighted the command words, key topics/issues and hooks, follow the following four steps:

➜ **Definitions and decision** — what is your decision and what terms do you need to define?
➜ **Issues and examples** — what are the key issues you need to argue and what examples can you bring in?
➜ **Analysis and chains of reasoning** — what arguments are you going to make and how are you going to develop these?
➜ **Structure your answer** — how many paragraphs does this response need and what will you put in each paragraph?

Example plan and answer

This section takes one of the essay titles from page 55 and gives an example of how the question can be deconstructed into a small number of planning steps. It is then followed by an annotated example of an answer to the question.

Aiming for an A in A-level Business

Worked example 5.1

A business has recently started to use Elkington's Triple Bottom Line to assess its overall performance. To what extent do you think the business is likely to have higher profits as a result of this?

Essay plan

Step 1: Definitions and decision

- Define Elkington's Triple Bottom Line.
- Decision is that it is more likely to result in a fall in profits in the short term.

Step 2: Issues and examples

- TBL will add to costs.
- TBL could be used as a marketing strategy.
- TBL is becoming more important within the modern business world.
- TBL is not required by all businesses.
- Examples: Lush, John Lewis, Tesco, Ryanair, Primark.

Step 3: Chains of reasoning

Increase in costs:
- Workers will need to be paid more.
- Reduces profits unless higher wages can be passed on in higher costs.
- Will depend on the price elasticity of demand for the business.
- Switching to fair trade/more ethical materials is normally more expensive (Lush).

Marketing strategy:
- Can utilise TBL as a USP, leading to a differentiated product, leading to higher prices and potentially higher profits.
- Will depend on the nature of the market and expectations of customers.
- Can be good for PR and attract customers (Lush/John Lewis).

Not required by all businesses:
- Will actually add to costs and reduce profits.
- Not required if customers don't expect it (Primark/Ryanair).
- Therefore unlikely to increase profits if consumers aren't concerned about it.

(Note: At this step, a selection has been made among the possible issues and examples listed at Step 2.)

Step 4: Structure

This answer should be written with 5 paragraphs:
- Introduction
- Point 1 — yes it could lead to higher profits
- Point 2 — yes it could
- Point 3 — no, actually likely to lower profts
- Conclusion — judgement

Annotated example 5.2

Below is an example of an essay response which is based on the plan shown in worked example 5.1. The question is repeated for convenience.

A business has recently started to use Elkington's Triple Bottom Line to assess its overall performance. To what extent do you think the business is likely to have higher profits as a result of this?

Elkington's Triple Bottom Line (TBL) is a business approach that looks at the following 3 Ps: Profit, People and Planet. The idea of this approach has become more popular in recent years as firms consider the CSR (Corporate Social Responsibilities) that they have and so no longer are they purely focusing on making a profit, but doing so in a responsible way. While focusing on the TBL can provide benefits to a firm, it does tend to raise costs, particularly in the short term, and so it is more likely to lead to reduced profits rather than higher profits in the main.

However, there are plenty of examples where the introduction of TBL can lead to higher profits. For example, the cosmetics company Lush has placed great emphasis on the planet aspect of the approach — it ensures that all of its raw materials are ethically sourced and aims to use renewable resources that are sustainable. While these tend to be relatively more expensive and add to the firm's costs, the company operates within a niche segment of the cosmetic industry, where its customers are willing to pay a premium price for the products, and so the company faces relatively price inelastic demand. This enables the firm to sustain high profit margins and gain a reputation for the people aspect of its operations, which has helped with the marketing and positioning of the product. This has generated an excellent reputation for the firm, which has arguably led to an increase in profits by adopting a TBL approach. Therefore this would support the view that being ethical and using TBL can lead to higher profits.

Concise and precise definition of TBL — sticks to the plan of starting with a definition.

Signalling where the response is heading — it can lead to higher profits but is more likely to lead to reduced profits. Note how this shows the benefit of having a clear plan and direction.

Bringing in an example of a company that has benefited. Nice example — not telling a story, but explaining how it has increased profits.

Really good chain of analysis which builds up a sustained line of reasoning. Linked to first planned argument.

Final sentence refers directly back to the question — evaluation as you go is always a good idea.

Likewise, the John Lewis partnership, which owns retail stores and the supermarket chain Waitrose, has always placed great emphasis on the treatment of its workers (partners). John Lewis has always looked to pay its workers above the average for the industry. While this would suggest that it would receive lower profits, the firm benefits in a number of ways. Firstly, the higher pay will tend to attract a greater pool of available workers, which will allow the firm to select the best candidates. In addition, treating its workers well with good working conditions results in a lower labour turnover figure, causing the firm to spend less on recruitment and training costs, which in the long run will potentially lead to lower staffing costs and allow the firm to achieve potentially higher profits. This is aligned also with the nature of the products and the way John Lewis positions itself. By having more experienced and arguably friendlier staff, it will attract customers who are willing to pay a slightly higher price for its products because the customer service and overall ambience within a John Lewis store are different as the firm is factoring in more than just the bottom line to its decision making. Therefore, by considering the people aspect of the TBL, firms like John Lewis can actually benefit from higher profits.

It is, however, important to realise that introducing the TBL will not be beneficial for all businesses. Some businesses pride themselves on offering a cost leadership strategy and are simply focused on providing products/services for the lowest cost possible. Customers are aware of this angle and will often choose to use businesses simply on a price basis and not factor in how ethical a business is. This can be seen in the airline industry where Ryanair offers very low ticket prices and still sees high demand

Analysis is excellent — sustained line of argument making great use of connectives.

Example is used well and shows insight and a developed line of argument 2 put forward in the plan.

Again, drawing argument back to the actual question — does it lead to higher profits?

Setting up a counter-argument — good balance and showing the benefit of having a plan for the response.

Annotated example 5.2

for its tickets, despite showing very little consideration for the people or planet aspects of the TBL. If it were to adopt Elkington's approach this would almost certainly lead to a fall in profits, as customers still expect low prices and it will become difficult to pass on the higher costs associated with paying staff higher wages (people) as the airline industry is very price elastic. It will also be difficult to change the perception and positioning of Ryanair to a slightly more expensive airline in the eyes of the customers, who tend to choose the airline on the basis of price and punctuality, rather than the level of customer service. Therefore, it will be a challenge for many businesses, especially those that have always had a focus on profits, to shift their focus towards the TBL and still enjoy the same level of profitability.

Excellent application and analysis of the point. Clearly thinking about the business context and the question itself.

Nicely supported judgement which links back to the question.

In conclusion, the introduction of TBL will have varying impacts on businesses — depending on the nature of the industry they operate in and the reputation they have. In industries where firms can utilise the TBL as a way to promote and make their brand stand out and gain from positive PR, it can be an effective way of increasing profits. This is especially the case in niche markets where there is a higher demand for products that are made in a way that considers the planet and the people who make them. However, within a highly competitive mass market, I believe that bringing in the TBL is going to be more challenging to implement. In the short term it is likely to lead to significantly higher costs as workers and suppliers need to be paid more. This will cut into the profit margins earned

A clear final judgement that brings together the different arguments previously put forward. Focus is on the question throughout.

by the firm and so it is much more likely that firms will actually suffer from lower profits by introducing the TBL and so will need to consider carefully before adopting the approach for their particular business.

Overall comments: This is a very balanced and focused response. It starts with a clear definition of Elkington's Triple Bottom Line and sets out what it is going to argue. The three arguments are well developed with clear chains of reasoning and with relevant examples that are chosen and used well. The final judgement states a clear position from the writer's point of view.

One point of note is that two arguments are given to support the idea that it will lead to higher profits, whereas only one argument is presented against. However, this argument is given greater weighting in the overall judgement. This is fine, but normally it might be expected that the overall judgement would follow the general balance of the response.

Overall, this candidate has clearly answered the question set and demonstrated a strong grasp of the key assessment objectives.

Activity

Produce your own detailed plans for the following essay titles:

- With the UK economy starting to enter the recovery phase, Waitrose could continue to focus on making its prices competitive, or look to increase its use of promotional methods.

  Evaluate these two options and recommend which option is more likely to increase the sales revenue of Waitrose.
- To what extent could Starbucks be viewed as a successful organisation? Justify your view.
- Evaluate the impact of introducing lean production practices on businesses and their stakeholders.
- To what extent is China an attractive market for all businesses wanting to sell their products internationally?

The importance of evaluation

The essay response in annotated example 5.2 shows a really strong structure. It is clear what the candidate is arguing in each paragraph — this student has taken on the skills learnt in the shorter responses and built on these to showcase their expertise in meeting all the asessment objectives. This is very important as all of the exams now use a levelled-response mark scheme. What this means is that examiners will make judgements about your competence in the four key skills, deciding whether they are 'limited', 'reasonable', 'good' or 'excellent'. Arguably the hardest one to show excellence in is evaluation.

Evaluation requires a clear final judgement, but it has to be based on the arguments that have been presented previously. Under the pressure of the exam hall, students all too frequently fail to bring the arguments together at the end — either through a lack of time, or simply because they do not really understand what the examiners are looking for.

So how and when should you evaluate? There is a definite argument that you should evaluate points as you go along — in this way, if you run out of time, then you will still have shown the examiner that you are evaluating and making judgements. However, the bulk of your justification should come at the end of your answer. This will demonstrate that you are able to make a decision and back it up.

You must also ensure that you are responding precisely to the actual question set. It is very easy to go off on a tangent, which will lead to the examiner writing the dreaded three letters NAQ on your script — Not Answering Question. A good tip is to re-read the question after every paragraph that you write to ensure that your response, while considering other factors, is still relevant and focused on exactly what the question has asked.

It is also worth considering some approaches to evaluation that you could utilise in your responses. In your lessons you may have been instructed to follow a mnemonic such as DISCO-M, AJIM or PECAN PIE. While these are all worthy of credit and can be very useful, as always they only really work effectively if you use them to answer the question directly. The danger is that they can become rather formulaic, which makes the response lose the individuality of the writer.

Below you will find example plans and annotated essays for two further essay questions.

Worked example 5.2

This example gives a sample plan for our second essay question (from annotated example 5.1 on page 55).

To what extent is the nature of the product the most important influence on the marketing mix of all businesses?

Essay plan

Step 1: Definitions and decision

- Define marketing mix.
- Decision is that product will be crucial for most businesses but not all.

Step 2: Issues and examples

- Product dictates the other aspects of the mix.
- Promotion can sometimes be more influential.
- Distribution can be more important for some markets.
- Price can arguably be more influential.
- Examples: Apple, Amazon, Lego, Primark, Airbnb, Aldi, VW, Costa.

Step 3: Chains of reasoning

Product is the most important:
- The product, e.g. iPhone/Tesla, dictates all other aspects of the mix.
- Will influence pricing strategy, distribution and promotion.
- Get the product right and everything else will fall into place.

Promotion is more significant:
- Sometimes inferior products will succeed due to the promotion.
- Hype and buzz can be more influential — Yeezy trainers.

Distribution:
- Having more outlets available and closer to customers will be more important — you might perceive other coffee products to be better quality but you choose the easiest option.

Price:
- In many cases, products can be fairly uniform, so the most important aspect is the price. A plain white T-shirt will be selected on price, not the brand.

Step 4: Structure

This answer should be written with 6 paragraphs:
- Introduction
- Point 1 — yes, product is the most influential
- Point 2 — no, promotion is more influential
- Point 3 — no, distribution (place) is more influential
- Point 4 — no, for many products price is the most influential
- Conclusion — judgement

Annotated example 5.3

Below is an example of an essay response which is based on the plan shown in worked example 5.2. The question is repeated for convenience.

To what extent is the nature of the product the most important influence on the marketing mix of all businesses?

The marketing mix is made up of 7 components, with Product, Price, Promotion and Distribution (Place) being significant aspects of this mix. The idea is that for any product or service to be successful, a business must devise a strategy that combines these different factors together to present a viable offering to consumers. In many ways, the nature of the product will be the most influential aspect, as for the majority of businesses this dictates the other parts of the mix. However, it would be incorrect to say that this was the case for all businesses.

Good precise definition. Some of the specifications include the 7 Ps but all expect you to know the 4 Ps stated here.

Clear direction about where the essay is heading and the likely overall judgement is stated early.

Where the product can be seen to be very important is with the case of the iPhone. Since being introduced to the market, the product has gained considerable market share from rival phones. This is because, while there are other smartphones available, the operating system, together with the applications and ease of use, has given the product a huge amount of brand loyalty and favourable reviews from customers. The development of newer models fits in with the idea of the product life cycle and the need to either extend the life cycle of certain versions or create new products. With such a fast-moving technological industry, having the most advanced product is crucial to success and means that the product can be promoted and priced to take into consideration the new features. Therefore in this case, it is very much the product that will influence the overall marketing mix. ←

Nice paragraph fully explaining the significance of product within a relevant context. Possibly slightly more development of analysis could have been achieved here.

However, while product is significant, it could also be argued that at times promotion of products is more important. In the mobile phone industry, there have been a number of very good products on a technical level, but these products have not been able to benefit from the level of promotional spending that Apple and Samsung can put behind their new products and so customers fail to become aware of just how technically superior these devices might be to others on the market. The power of promotion can also be seen with the case of trainers and sportswear whereby it is the advertising and promotion of the brand that is more important to success rather than the product itself. This can be seen with certain trainers having a much higher selling price, despite offering few (if any) additional features. In this market segment, it is invariably the brand and how it is promoted, rather than the product itself, that is most important. ←

First counter-argument about how other factors are more significant. Uses same context as previous paragraph at start and then brings in a relevant further context that clearly shows promotion being of greater significance than the product itself.

It is also the case that for some markets, the distribution network becomes more important than the product itself. This can be seen in the case of the coffee market, where firms such as Starbucks and Costa place as much significance on the locations of their outlets as they do on the quality of the coffee they sell. This is because the firms know that the greater the number of outlets they have, the more likely they are to attract customers, and in particular, if they can monopolise a particular location such as an airport or railway station, then customers will be forced to choose them regardless of how much they like or rate the quality of the coffee served. Having many locations also means that the reputation of the brand increases and reaches more customers and so the firms can look to extend their distribution network even further. The success of the large multinationals, such as McDonald's and Coca-Cola, has been built upon their ability to reach a large global audience far more than on the overall quality of their burgers and drinks respectively. In both cases, there are arguably higher-quality versions of the product itself, which therefore proves that the product is not the most important aspect of the marketing mix.

It is almost certainly the case that, in some situations, far more important than the product is the price. For many customers, this is most certainly the defining factor. This can be seen with the growth of low-cost supermarkets, with customers now making their decision of where to shop based primarily on price. When it comes to the difference between staple products such as milk, potatoes or plain white T-shirts, consumers tend to be less brand-loyal and are far more concerned with the price. These generic products do not lend themselves to brand differentiation and consumers are likely to be unable to distinguish between the product quality of different brands, and so marketing decisions will be less about the individual product, and more

An insightful line of argument that uses some very good examples and offers a really good argument that product is not the most important aspect.

about the supermarkets as a whole. The general slowdown in economic growth across the world in the last decade has meant that consumers have become more price and income elastic in their decision making, and so Aldi and Lidl have been able to focus on providing the staple products at low prices and low profit margins, which has been the most important aspect of their marketing mix. However, at the same time, they have had to work hard on changing consumers' perceptions that low price equates with low-quality products. This shows that firms do still need to consider the product alongside the other elements of the mix, but it is not the most important influence in this situation. ◄——

Therefore, while product does constitute one of the most significant influences of the marketing mix, it is incorrect to say that it is the most important influence for all businesses. This is because the marketing mix is just that, a combination of factors that need to work together and complement each of the other factors. It will always depend on the business, the industry and the target market that the product is being aimed at. This suggests that getting the product right is very important, but while it does dictate the other elements in lots of ways, the relative significance of the product will vary. ◄——

Another strong paragraph that brings in other external aspects that will influence the marketing mix and not just internal factors. Thus relevant theory and concepts are used well without losing focus on the actual question set.

Candidate has evaluated throughout the response and brings each paragraph back to the question set. The final conclusion brings together previous arguments and clearly justifies their viewpoint.

Overall comments: This is a response that clearly benefits from sticking to the plan set out. Focus on the question is consistent throughout and there is insightful use of a range of relevant examples. The chains of analysis could be stronger in places, but overall the use of theories, application and constant evaluation throughout the response makes this an A-grade response. Each paragraph has a purpose and a developed line of argument that addresses the issues raised in the question.

Worked example 5.3

This example gives a sample plan for our third essay question (from annotated example 5.1 on page 55).

To what extent are the demand on and costs of a business mainly determined by factors outside of its control?

Essay plan

Step 1: Definitions and decision

- Define demand and costs.
- Define external factors.
- Some businesses very dependent on external factors — but will still depend on how well the business is run internally.

Step 2: Issues and examples

    Factors influencing demand — nature of the product and level of competition.
- Costs — influences and issues — links to margins and competitiveness.
- PESTEL factors and how important these are.
- Examples: car industry, house building, technology firms, supermarkets.

Step 3: Chains of reasoning

Influences on demand:
- Link to external factors such as seasonality and economic factors.

Costs involved:
- Costs can be controlled — but depends on Porter and buyer/supplier power.
- Will depend on the size of the business and the market segment.

PESTEL factors:
- Other external factors might be more important.
- Will also depend on how the business is run internally.
- Develop arguments in relation to social factors and possibly technology?

Step 4: Structure

This answer should be written with 6 paragraphs:
- Introduction
- Point 1 — yes: demand will be significantly influenced by external factors
- Point 2 — yes and no: costs can be influenced by external factors but firms do have some control
- Point 3 — yes: external factors will have a significant impact on the costs and demand
- Point 4 — no: internal factors are arguably just as important
- Conclusion — judgement

Annotated example 5.4

Below is an example of an essay response which is based on the plan shown in worked example 5.3. The question is repeated for convenience.

To what extent are the demand on and costs of a business mainly determined by factors outside of its control?

The demand a business faces will come from consumers who are willing and able to pay for the product/service that they provide. The business will also face two main types of costs: fixed (which do not vary with output) and variable (which vary directly with the amount produced/sold). It could be argued that in the short term a business will be able to have greater flexibility in terms of variable costs as it can relatively easily switch suppliers of raw material as required, whereas it will be harder to alter/renegotiate fixed costs such as overheads in the short run. However, the full impact of these external factors on the business will depend on the sector that it operates in, together with how well the firm is run internally as to how it can cope with issues outside of its control.

Excellent introduction. Precise and to-the-point definitions together with a clear understanding of exactly what the requirements of the question are.

In terms of demand, certain businesses will be very dependent on seasonality factors and the current state of the economy. A good example of this would be the travel and airline industry. These businesses will be invariably seasonal and the demand for their products will be at a peak in the summer months and, to a lesser extent, the winter months — but essentially demand will be high whenever there is a holiday period and lower during school term times. This means that the businesses will realise that they face relatively more price inelastic demand during the holiday periods and much more elastic demand during the off-peak periods. Therefore, firms will need to be able to adapt to these changes in demand and look to price their products accordingly. This means that higher prices are charged when the products are in high demand. However, the hotels

Good recognition of factors that are likely to influence demand and nice application to relevant sectors. Potentially could have looked at factors that influence price elasticity of demand.

that companies like Thomas Cook deal with are also well aware of the nature of demand and are likely to increase their prices and so the costs involved for the business will be higher also. The state of the economy will also play a significant role. Customers will tend to look to book more overseas holidays when the pound is relatively strong, as this will mean that imports (the costs of the holidays) are relatively cheap, and this will often lead to a surge in demand. The uncertainty of the recent Brexit decision has led to the pound becoming weaker — particularly against the euro — and so holiday firms offering vacations inside the EU have seen the demand fall significantly, whereas areas such as Croatia (outside the EU) have seen demand increase. While the firms can look to react and offer more holidays in non-EU destinations, it is extremely difficult to increase hotel capacity and available flights immediately and so the demand for holidays is clearly an area that is often determined by factors beyond the control of the business itself.

The recession and state of the economy within the EU has been an issue facing all businesses. With a general lower level of demand across industries, this has led to costs falling in the main as suppliers become more concerned about securing contracts. This has helped firms but they have also been then forced to pass these cost savings on to customers in the form of lower prices because customers have become more price sensitive as their disposable incomes have been reduced and overall consumer confidence has decreased. This has represented a good opportunity for counter-cyclical businesses such as low-cost airlines and budget supermarkets who have seen an increase in the demand for their products as they tend to thrive more when the level of economic activity is lower.

On the other hand, car companies have seen a significant fall in the demand for their new

Topical and relevant example and another clear argument about what factors will impact on demand.

The two arguments within the paragraph are drawn together to show a relevant judgement in relation to the question set.

Using the point about economic factors but now relating them to costs. Candidate has clearly identified the hooks and is looking to discuss both demand and costs. This is excellent technique.

vehicles as people are less likely to spend on a big-ticket item such as a car. This, together with the fact that cars are built to a better standard and last longer these days, means that the demand for new vehicle registrations has fallen over the last few years, whereas the second-hand market for cars has seen a surge in demand. These external factors are prevalent in many industries — an example where businesses recognise their significance is in the estate agent industry. These firms seek to protect themselves by both offering new houses to purchase as well as having a rental section, as they realise that the state of the economy and the level of house purchasing will be mainly determined by economic factors such as the interest rate and monetary policy decisions by central government, rather than what they can control themselves. By offering two distinct products the estate agents guard against being fully susceptible to issues outside of their control — but are a very good example of a business that will see demand influenced by outside factors.

Back on focusing on demand factors but again showing nice application to two different market segments that will be heavily influenced by factors outside of their control.

There are also firms that do not need to worry too much about economic factors in terms of demand as they carry such importance that demand will always stay constant in the main. Firms such as Apple have been on an upward trend in terms of demand for their products since they launched their first iPhone. Sales have increased consistently, despite the overall poor external conditions in the main. Their success, while not an isolated case, actually proves that it is how a business is run internally that is far more significant to its overall performance. While the company needs to keep aware of the latest technological developments within the industry (an external issue), the way the company operates and approaches and reacts to the external changes internally is a more significant factor in the demand and overall success of the business. Apple is able to use its previous success to attract new software developers, which helps it maintain a competitive advantage, and highly skilled designers, who allow it to keep launching new and innovative products to market. Apple is also able to exert considerable power and influence over its suppliers as manufacturers of component parts want to secure the contract. This helps the company keep costs low, which helps it to increase its profit margins and still thrive in a marketplace that has seen more competition enter the segment, but fail to take over the dominant position that Apple has been able to establish.

Therefore, in conclusion, while external factors clearly do have an impact on the demand and costs of a business, it is my view that firms that are lean and run well can adapt and be flexible in relation to these issues outside of their control. It does require good leadership and a workforce that can react quickly and effectively and this does rely on communication within the organisation being strong, but overall, the majority of businesses will know that they are always going to be influenced by external factors, and it is how they respond to and deal with these that will be the biggest influence on their long-term success. Therefore, firms can influence the demand and costs they face by their position within the industry, and so to suggest that it is mainly determined by outside factors is not correct in my opinion as ultimately the business decides on its marketing mix and positioning of products and this is probably the main determinant of demand. As for costs, a successful firm should look to have a degree of control and a choice of different suppliers and therefore not be forced to buy from just one monopolistic supplier in the main.

Nice counter-argument that is developing the line that while external factors will impact businesses such as Apple, they can still control these to some extent. This is a clever reworking of the focus of the question and shows a candidate who has thought about the key issues and benefited from having a plan.

This is a clear, final judgement that is supported well.

Overall comments: This is a very thorough response that covers a wide range of arguments but always links them back to the actual question set. There is effective interweaving of examples to support the lines of analysis. The candidate tends to focus more on demand factors but does cover the cost issues as well, so is picking up on the hooks within the question. The response clearly knows where it is going and what it is looking to argue and then does it. This is invariably the hallmark of an A*/A-grade response.

Activity

Of the six essay titles on page 55, we have provided examples of detailed plans and annotated essay responses for the first three. Using the planning steps given on page 56 as a template, develop plans and essay responses for the final three questions.

Final thoughts

While the evaluation questions are very important in terms of the number of marks that they are worth, they are not so difficult once you have broken down the question into the component parts, as the above examples have shown. What is vital is that you keep in mind, throughout your response, the key skills you need to demonstrate — that is, knowledge, application, analysis and, in these questions, evaluation.

Examiners are looking for a response that answers directly the question that has been asked. Therefore, make sure that you devote some time to planning your response, and that you then make effective use of your plan when you are writing your response to ensure that you are not drifting away from the question.

If you re-read the annotated examples in this chapter, you should notice that they never waver from the actual question and at the end of each paragraph demonstrate that they are directly responding and evaluating the arguments in relation to the question. If you can do this, then you are well on the way to an A*/A grade — but remember that this is not going to happen overnight and you need to practise and develop your essay-writing skills over the 2-year course.

You should know

> **The first step in answering an essay question is to deconstruct the question to identify the hooks and exactly what you are being asked to respond to.**
> **For essay questions you are expected to demonstrate *all* of the key assessment objectives.**
> **It is vital to devote time to planning your response, so you can structure it effectively.**
> **Remember to make effective use of your plan when writing your essay to help you keep focused on the question.**
> **Responses that evaluate points throughout *and* at the end maximise your chances of picking up key evaluation marks.**

Aiming for an A in A-level Business

6 Exam skills

Ideally you should not be leaving your exam preparation to the final few weeks before the exams themselves. If you have gleaned anything from this guide, it is the need to be prepared and focused throughout the course and realise that the work you put in over the 2 years of the course will have a cumulative benefit for your overall performance.

This chapter provides guidance for your final exam preparation and for the exam itself. However, the information about revision techniques will also be useful during earlier stages of your course.

Before the exam

The first and most important thing to do is to find out exactly when your exams are set to take place and see how these fit in with your other subjects. While you are likely to receive a personalised exam timetable from your school or college, there is nothing to stop you getting ahead of the game. The exam boards publish draft timetables a year in advance and these do not change significantly. The three or four papers that you are scheduled to sit are normally spaced out over 10 to 12 days.

You need to be confident that you understand the exact structure of your exams, what areas of the syllabus they will examine and the style of questions you will be facing. Details of the exam papers set by the different exam boards are given in the final section of the guide, 'Exam board focus' (see page 81).

Revision techniques

There are a number of different revision techniques available and individuals may vary as to which they find most effective. However, there are clearly some methods that are far more advantageous than others. The pyramid in Figure 6.1 shows how various methods differ in terms of the rate of retention of what is learnt.

 Exam tip

One of the challenges of A-level study is that you will be tested on your recall of topics from 2 years of work. Therefore to help with your revision you need to get your folders in order and laid out in a way that makes reviewing your work easier to do. You are likely to have been given an overview of your exam board specification at the start of your course. This should be the starting point for your revision as the examiners can only ever ask questions which are directly linked to the specification.

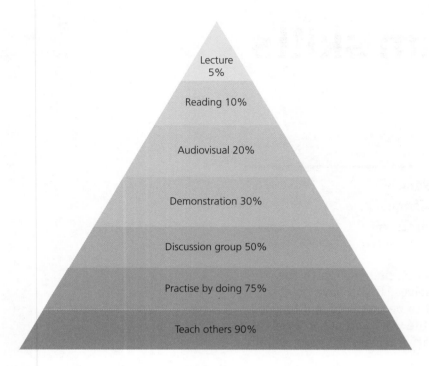

Figure 6.1 Rates of learning retention for different revision methods

This shows that just re-reading previously taken notes will not be very effective as a way of revising what you have been taught. It is far better to turn your revision into an active project and look to create meaningful resources or engage in activities that are likely to further your understanding.

It is a good idea to make new notes so that you are bringing together the different topics that you have covered. Depending on your preference, you could do this in the form of flashcards, spider diagrams, bullet-point notes or essay plans. Revision is not about learning new things — rather, it is about 'reviewing' what you have already learnt in a way that is meaningful and useful for answering the questions that you are likely to face.

Definitions

A good starting point is to create a revision resource that ensures you have all of the key terms defined and learnt. Remember that these are the gatekeepers for nearly all of the questions that you are likely to face. There are a substantial number of these terms, so it will be very useful to have a glossary which sets them out in a form that you can readily access and use. It might be a good idea to invest in a set of index cards or create your own set of flashcards that you can use to test both yourself and your classmates.

Case studies

One of the most effective ways to revise is to take the top ten industries suggested on page 11, look for specific examples of businesses within these industries and build up a mini fact file for each business, making links to particular areas of the syllabus. Then, for each example business, you can build up an analytical paragraph that can be used within your longer responses. Several worked examples are given below as illustration.

> **! Common pitfall**
>
> Candidates often let easy marks slip away by offering 'woolly', imprecise definitions. Make sure you are really confident about using all the key terms — one or two extra marks really can make the difference between grades.

Worked example 6.1

Industry: fashion retail

Example: Zara
- Largest clothing retailer in the world
- Industry very fast-moving
- Zara focuses on very lean operations — replicates items from the catwalk to the shop in less than 2 weeks
- Manufacturing mainly within the EU — higher cost but quicker delivery times
- Turns stock over very quickly — monitors what is selling and stocks more
- Most fashion retailers stock for four seasons — Zara changes stock twice a week and customers visit stores more frequently
- Zero advertising — quality of clothes and reasonable prices make advertising redundant
- Culture focused on maximum efficiency
- Leadership — Ortega, one of the richest men in the world
- Multinational company — has successfully exploited emerging markets — Ansoff market development
- Recruits the best designers in the industry
- Kaizen — continuously improving operations

Zara is an example of a company that has focused on the operations management aspect to gain a competitive advantage over other firms within the industry. By recruiting the best designers, the company can replicate the latest trends really quickly, so its products are always on trend. This means that customers are likely to visit the stores more frequently, which increases footfall significantly, resulting in increased sales. All this gives the company brand loyalty and repeat custom, enabling it to maintain a dominant position within the industry. By minimising waste, the company keeps its costs under control, which allows it to charge competitive prices but maintain a healthy profit margin.

Worked example 6.2

Industry: food retail

Example: Costa
- Owned by Whitbread, former brewery that used to run pubs, restaurants and hotels
- Company moved out of brewing due to increased competition and not being able to exploit economies of scale of rival firms
- Recognised growth of coffee industry and success of Starbucks
- Changed strategy and moved into coffee and away from beer
- Targeted railway and airport terminals initially — lower price elasticity of demand
- Developed brand and moved into town and city centres and retail parks
- Now the number one coffee chain in the UK and second largest in the world
- Product is in high demand — large profit margins and low unit cost
- UK now a nation of coffee drinkers rather than tea drinkers

✓ Exam tip

Having to hand up-to-date examples is very useful. While you will be given case study questions and data to use, having a bank of examples that can be used to compare and contrast really makes an A*/A candidate stand out.

Whitbread recognised that it needed to adapt its strategy as it was struggling to compete in the brewing industry — it could not keep its unit costs as low as its bigger competitors due to not being able to fully exploit economies of scale. Whitbread recognised that the coffee industry was

➡

just entering the growth stage of the product life cycle and shifted its focus on to developing a brand and chain of coffee houses throughout the UK. By targeting transport hubs initially, it recognised that consumers had less choice in those locations and were willing to pay a higher price for their coffee. This allowed whitbread to enjoy larger profit margins, which then allowed it to reinvest its profits into expanding and growing its chain more quickly. It was also able to use the experience of the distribution of products around the UK via its old restaurant network and adapt and modify this into its coffee operations.

Worked example 6.3

Industry: gaming consoles

Example: Nintendo
- Industry dominated by three firms
- Nintendo — targeting slightly different segments — popular with younger consumers (DS) and also attracted female segment (Wii)
- Product life cycle — console development and sales typically 5 to 7 years
- Need to innovate and introduce new technology
- High R&D budget — along with promotional spend
- Brand loyalty important but very dependent on the quality of the product. Tends to price its consoles lower than rivals Sony and Microsoft
- Matching demand to meet supply — global operations but mainly manufacturing in high-cost Japan
- Strategy — Pokémon GO — very popular and embraced latest technology — hard to maintain competitive advantage for long — competitors watch closely the actions of rivals

Nintendo is a company constantly focusing on innovation and research and development of new products to try and maintain its market share in a fiercely competitive oligopolistic marketplace. It is the smallest of the three firms operating within the console market and has to look to develop USPs that keep its products relevant and in demand. It has done this by focusing on specific market segments and its products are often chosen as the entry-level console for young children and families. It targets and positions its products to take advantage of this segment and produce games and consoles with a more 'fun' element. The company realises that as gamers get more serious they may switch to rival brands, but it aims to squeeze as much profit as possible from consumers who are new to gaming, and with innovations such as motion controllers, it has led the way in recent years. However, it is very difficult to constantly come up with new innovations. This requires considerable investment with no guarantee of success, which means that it remains difficult for firms such as Nintendo to stay competitive.

Discussing with others

Once you have completed fact files and exemplar paragraphs, an excellent way to develop your understanding further is to talk to other students within your class and compare examples and notes. This will not only enable you to further build up your case studies and your knowledge, but also help you to consider how you could improve your own examples. It is a good idea to share these materials — not only does this cut your workload, but by working together, you can further refine and improve your case studies. It is likely that your classmates will have suggestions for what you could add to make your case study even better.

Look again at the learning retention rates shown in Figure 6.1 (page 74). By demonstrating your examples you are likely to retain 30%, by discussing with others 50% — and by teaching others why and how you have used an example, the retention rate increases to 90%. Therefore, you need to make revision an active exercise rather than just sitting in your room re-reading your own notes.

Practising by doing

The fact file and example paragraph revision exercise is a great example of practising by doing. You are looking to put what you have learnt into practice, in the context of the exam skills that you will be tested on. When putting together your fact file, remember that you are trying to demonstrate, at all times, the key skills of subject knowledge, application to a particular case study, and then analysing and building up an argument. The skill that you are not necessarily able to showcase in this way is that of evaluation and this is where the need to access past papers is so important.

The single best way to revise and prepare for the exams themselves is to tackle actual exam papers. You need to try and replicate as much as possible the conditions that you will face within the exam hall. The exam board websites have numerous past papers, specimen papers, mark schemes and examiner reports that you can access. These are, quite simply, a huge asset for you.

The examiner reports are always full of tips about what examiners are looking for and, perhaps more importantly, what they are not looking for. You should read through these and pick out the key learning points about what students have done well in the past and the areas where they have struggled. The reports will go through each question in detail. Reading them *before* you attempt the past paper questions should help you to avoid the errors that previous students have made.

One of the challenges of the exams is the length and duration of the papers. At the start of your revision, it is unlikely that you will be dedicating a whole 2 hours of your time to tackling one of the papers. You are more likely to attempt single questions at a time, and while this is useful, it is important that you keep an eye on the bigger picture of the exam itself.

You want to prepare for the exams in a similar fashion to someone preparing for their first marathon. The idea when training for a marathon is to build up slowly the number of miles you complete. Over the months of training, you increase the number of miles you complete in each training session and gradually build up to about 22 miles, before tapering down as the day of the event itself approaches. You should be looking to do the same in terms of your revision.

! Common pitfall

When working with others it is very easy to lose focus on what you should be doing. Group work can often mean 'no work' for some individuals. It is important that you team up with like-minded students who recognise the benefit of sharing good practice and ideas. You don't want to be carrying any 'passengers' who fail to contribute.

! Common pitfall

The two most common pitfalls for students in the exam are misreading the wording of the question and simply running out of time.

At the same time, you need to keep your revision relevant and time-constrained. There is no point in spending 50 minutes on a practice 20-mark question, when in the exam you are only likely to have 25 minutes maximum. Therefore, when attempting questions from past papers, always set yourself a time limit, in order to replicate the conditions that you will face in the exam itself. It is highly likely that you will exceed this on the first few attempts, but over time you will get better at keeping your writing succinct and to the point, and will be able to manage your time much more effectively.

The exam itself
Before you go in

It is important to sleep well the night before the exam. Staying up into the early hours is counter-productive. You are facing 2 hours of intense concentration and writing and therefore you need to be rested so that you can focus your energy on the exam itself.

You should also make sure you have correctly fuelled your body. Breakfast is quite rightly described as the most important meal of the day and this is true whether your exam is in the morning or in the afternoon. You must give your brain and your body the required fuel for the journey ahead. If you are planning a long road trip and only have enough fuel for the first 30 miles, then you are going to have to stop and disrupt your journey early on and this is going to hold you back. Therefore, make sure you are ready and focused by fuelling up.

As to last-minute revision, this is arguably counter-productive. You need to realise that you have worked hard in your preparation and that the work is done. Frantically looking at notes as you go into the exam hall is rarely likely to be helpful. It is far better to just remind yourself of the structure of the exam and the likely types of question that you will face.

In terms of what you need to take into the exam hall, this has probably been covered many times by your teachers and exam officers. As a minimum you should have in your clear pencil case:
→ pens (at least four)
→ highlighters
→ pencil
→ ruler
→ eraser
→ calculator

It is also important to make sure that you are using a pen that you are comfortable with. You might have been using gel pens for the 2 years of your course, but in the exams themselves, you must use a black ballpoint pen. The reason for this is that your responses on paper are scanned in by computer and gel pens can sometimes leak through the pages, making the work very difficult to read and mark. Therefore, you really should practise writing with the style of pen that you are likely to be using as you will become more accustomed to it. Remember that you will be writing for up to 2 hours and you want to make this experience as comfortable as possible.

Managing your time

While the exam papers are laid out in a considered manner and typically start with shorter questions before building up to more analytical and evaluative longer questions, it really is the case that you do not need to answer the questions in sequential order. This is particularly useful to know if you struggle with managing your timing. The mock exams that you face in the run-up to the exam will give you an idea as to how well you manage your time under the pressures of the exam hall.

It is *always* advisable to skim-read the whole exam paper to give you an idea of the questions you are going to face. This will allow you to see the bigger picture and realise that there are some questions that are easy to tackle, with a few that you might find more challenging. This is the case for all exams and the best way to approach the questions is to attempt first the ones that you know you are going to be strong on. Knowing that you have picked up close to maximum marks on 50% of the paper will give you confidence for tackling the more challenging areas.

However, this advice only works if you are very well aware of the overall timing of the paper. The mark-a-minute rule is a very good rule of thumb as the majority of the exams are based on this. Factoring in reading time, you should be aiming to dedicate the same number of minutes to the question as the number of marks allocated to it. Remember that this does not mean spending all of that time writing. Factoring in planning and thinking time is essential.

You are also likely to be given a choice of questions on some of the exam papers. This is where the ability to stop, think and plan becomes crucial. The work that you have carried out in terms of planning out and structuring your essay responses will allow you to identify the hooks and key themes of the question set and tailor your response to fit them.

The ideal A*/A candidate is one who picks up marks consistently and steadily across all of the exam papers. Answering each and every question 'pretty well' is clearly a recipe for success. However, this is not always possible for every candidate and the weighting of the later questions means that if you run out of time and miss a particular question, this can significantly reduce your chances of achieving the top grades. In this scenario it might prove more sensible to have a strategy that guards against this.

In table 6.1, you can see how three different students approached an exam and how this affected their marks.

The table shows that running out of time is one of the biggest threats to your chances of getting an A*/A grade. The tactical student has opted to miss out one of the lower-tariff questions, realising that a strong performance on the longer-response questions is more important to their overall grade. While you really want to be aiming for the steady approach, the reality in the exam hall is that you are under pressure and so the need to practise your timing and approach once again becomes vital.

Table 6.1 How three different students scored in an exam

Marks available	Student A (steady Eddie)	Student B (Irene out of time)	Student C (tactical Trevor)
12 marks	8	10	0
12 marks	8	10	10
16 marks	12	14	14
16 marks	12	12	14
20 marks	14	8	17
24 marks	18	0	21
TOTAL	72	54	76

After the exam

Once you have completed an exam, the best thing you can do is try to forget about it! Business is a subject that does not always have a definitive answer for a question — and this is especially the case for the longer-response questions. As long as you have justified your view and supported it in relation to the question, your answer will be acceptable. It does not matter if you said the company was 'right' to adopt that strategy and a friend said they were 'wrong' — you can both be right and be picking up maximum marks.

As for the data questions, students will often come out and ask each other, for example, 'What did you get for the break-even question?' However, the reality is that this will not be worth much more than 3 marks out of 300. There is no need to fret if your response was different from someone else's — you are likely to have picked up marks anyway for stating the formula and it really is not worth worrying about.

You will have a general feel for how the exam went. If you think you could have managed your timings better, then try to learn from this for your next exam. If it is your last exam, then just try to relax and realise that you have worked your hardest and given it your best — that is all anyone can ask.

You should know

> Effective revision is not passive — revision needs to be personalised and active.
> Effective revision starts with learning key terms and definitions.
> Building up exemplar case studies and sharing and discussing them with others will help you retain your understanding more effectively.
> Practice makes perfect but it has to be meaningful practice.
> Effective management of timing is vital for success in the exam hall.

Exam board focus

Learning outcomes

> To understand the exam structure of each examination board
> To know how to prepare for your examination papers
> To know how to organise your notes for the different examination boards

The four examination boards cover similar but slightly different topics and each has a different way of structuring the exam papers and styling the questions. It is important to know that everything covered so far is equally applicable to all of the boards. However, you will need to understand the subtle nuances of difference between the boards in order to maximise your chances of achieving an A*/A grade. As outlined in the opening section of this guide ('About this book'), the percentage of candidates receiving an A*/A grade is much the same for each board and so it is not the case that one board is easier or harder than any other.

AQA paper structure
The papers
Paper 1
This paper is 2 hours long. It is worth a total of 100 marks and 33.3% of the A-level.

It consists of the following sections:

A. 15 × 1-mark multiple-choice questions
B. 35 marks — a mix of short-answer data questions for 17 marks plus 2 × 9-mark analyse questions
C. Choice of 1 essay out of 2 possible 25-mark essay questions
D. Choice of 1 essay out of 2 possible 25-mark essay questions

Note: Sections C and D will expect you to bring in your own relevant business examples that can be linked to the topic in the question.

Paper 2
This paper is 2 hours long. It is worth a total of 100 marks and 33.3% of the A-level.

There are three different compulsory case studies and compulsory questions.

For *each* case study, you are likely to face:

→ 1 or 2 data questions (3–4 marks maximum)
→ 1 × 9-mark analyse question
→ 1 × 16- or 20-mark evaluation-style question

Note: At least two of the evaluation-style questions will expect you to bring in business examples from outside of the case study material.

The approaches for the 16- and 20-mark questions are exactly the same — they should not be treated any differently.

Paper 3

This paper is 2 hours long. It is worth a total of 100 marks and 33.3% of the A-level.

There is one compulsory case study with data appendices and six compulsory questions:

→ 2 × 12-mark analyse questions
→ 2 × 16-mark evaluation questions
→ 1 × 20-mark evaluation question
→ 1 × 24-mark evaluation question

Note: At least one of the questions will expect you to bring in your own examples from outside of the case study material.

The 12-mark analyse questions should be treated in a similar way to the 9-mark analyse questions that you come across in Papers 1 and 2.

Analysis and evaluation

The table below gives a breakdown of questions that expect you to demonstrate analysis and evaluation in addition to knowledge and application.

Paper	Questions	Additional skills required	Number of marks
1	2 × 9 marks	Analysis	18 marks
	2 × 25 marks	Analysis and evaluation	50 marks
2	3 × 9 marks	Analysis	27 marks
	2 × 16 marks	Analysis and evaluation	32 marks
	1 × 20 marks	Analysis and evaluation	20 marks
3	2 × 12 marks	Analysis	24 marks
	2 × 16 marks	Analysis and evaluation	32 marks
	1 × 20 marks	Analysis and evaluation	20 marks
	1 × 24 marks	Analysis and evaluation	24 marks
Total marks			**247 marks out of 300 = 82%**

This table demonstrates the importance of the higher-order skills to your success. Remember, though, that you need to start with key definitions and understanding before you can showcase your analysis and evaluative skills.

Edexcel paper structure
The papers
Paper 1: Marketing, people and global businesses
This paper is 2 hours long. It is worth a total of 100 marks and 33.3% of the A-level.

There are two different compulsory case studies and compulsory questions.

For *each* case study, you are likely to face:
→ 2 × 4-mark knowledge/application questions
→ 1 × 10-mark analyse question
→ 1 × 12-mark analyse/evaluate question
→ 1 × 20-mark analyse/evaluate question

Paper 2: Business activities, decisions and strategy
This paper is 2 hours long. It is worth a total of 100 marks and 33.3% of the A-level.

There are two different compulsory case studies and compulsory questions.

For *each* case study, you are likely to face:
→ 2 × 4-mark knowledge/application questions
→ 1 × 10-mark analyse question
→ 1 × 12-mark analyse/evaluate question
→ 1 × 20-mark analyse/evaluate question

Note: Papers 1 and 2 share the same structure. They will have questions based on separate parts of the specification.

Neither paper will specifically ask you to bring in examples outside of those featured within the case study. However, you are expected to have an overall awareness of what is happening within the external business environment.

Paper 3: Investigating business in a competitive environment
This paper is 2 hours long. It is worth a total of 100 marks and 33.3% of the A-level.

Questions will be based on a pre-released case study. Notes are not allowed to be taken into the examination room, but it is expected that students will have conducted detailed background research into the particular topic.

There will be two sections of case study material that includes data on businesses relevant to the pre-release scenario. Each case study will feature the following style of questions:
→ 1 × 8-mark question — Analyse
→ 1 × 10-mark question — Analyse
→ 1 × 12-mark question — Analyse/evaluate
→ 1 × 20-mark question — Analyse/evaluate

Note: On Edexcel papers, you will only see questions that carry the following tariffs:

→ 4 marks — Knowledge/application
→ 8 marks — Analyse
→ 10 marks — Analyse
→ 12 marks — Analyse/evaluate
→ 20 marks — Analyse/evaluate

Analysis and evaluation

The table below gives a breakdown of questions that expect you to demonstrate analysis and evaluation in addition to knowledge and application.

Paper	Questions	Additional skills required	Number of marks
1	2 × 10 marks	Analysis	20 marks
	2 × 12 marks	Analysis and evaluation	24 marks
	2 × 20 marks	Analysis and evaluation	40 marks
2	2 × 10 marks	Analysis	20 marks
	2 × 12 marks	Analysis and evaluation	24 marks
	2 × 20 marks	Analysis and evaluation	40 marks
3	2 × 8 marks	Analysis	16 marks
	2 × 10 marks	Analysis	20 marks
	2 × 12 marks	Analysis and evaluation	24 marks
	2 × 20 marks	Analysis and evaluation	40 marks
Total marks			**268 marks out of 300 = 89%**

This table demonstrates the importance of the higher-order skills to your success. Remember, though, that you need to start with key definitions and understanding before you can showcase your analysis and evaluative skills.

OCR paper structure

The papers

Paper 1: Operating in a local business environment

This paper is 2 hours long. It is worth a total of 80 marks and 33.3% of the A-level.

It includes the following:

→ 15 × 1-mark multiple-choice questions — 15 marks

It also includes a compulsory case study with the following:

→ 4 × short-answer questions — 20 marks
→ 3 × 15-mark evaluate questions — 45 marks

Paper 2: The UK business environment

This paper is 2 hours long. It is worth a total of 80 marks and 33.3% of the A-level.

There is one compulsory case study with compulsory questions as follows:

➜ 8 or 9 short-answer questions testing knowledge and calculations — 32 marks

➜ 2 × 9-mark analyse questions — 18 marks

➜ 2 × 15-mark evaluate questions — 30 marks

Paper 3: The global business environment

This paper is 2 hours long. It is worth a total of 80 marks and 33.3% of the A-level.

There is one compulsory case study with compulsory questions as follows:

➜ 3 or 4 short-answer questions testing knowledge and calculations — 12 marks

➜ 3 × 6-mark analyse questions — 18 marks

➜ 1 × 10-mark evaluate question — 10 marks

➜ 2 × 20-mark evaluate questions — 40 marks

Analysis and evaluation

The table below gives a breakdown of questions that expect you to demonstrate analysis and evaluation in addition to knowledge and application.

Paper	Questions	Additional skills required	Number of marks
1	2 × 7 marks	Analysis	14 marks
	3 × 15 marks	Analysis and evaluation	45 marks
2	2 × 9 marks	Analysis	18 marks
	2 × 15 marks	Analysis and evaluation	30 marks
3	3 × 6 marks	Analysis	18 marks
	1 × 10 marks	Analysis	10 marks
	2 × 20 marks	Analysis and evaluation	40 marks
Total marks			**175 marks out of 240 = 73%**

This table demonstrates the importance of the higher-order skills to your success. Remember, though, that you need to start with key definitions and understanding before you can showcase your analysis and evaluative skills.

Eduqas paper structure

The Eduqas exams are exams offered by the Welsh examination board for students taking exams within English centres.

The papers

Paper 1: Business opportunities and functions

This paper is 2 hours 15 minutes long. It is worth a total of 80 marks and 33.3% of the A-level.

The exam features a number of compulsory case study questions and short-answer questions worth between 2 and 8 marks.

There are three slightly longer evaluative questions worth 12 marks each.

Paper 2: Business analysis and strategy

This paper is 2 hours 15 minutes long. It is worth a total of 80 marks and 33.3% of the A-level.

The exam features a number of compulsory case studies and compulsory questions but with a greater focus on calculations and interpretation of data.

For *each* case study, you are likely to face:

→ two or three data questions (3–4 marks maximum)

→ two or three 6- to 8-mark analyse questions

One of the case study questions will be worth 14 marks and will expect you to evaluate.

Paper 3: Business in a changing world

This paper is 2 hours 15 minutes long. It is worth a total of 80 marks and 33.3% of the A-level.

This paper involves:

→ one case study with five compulsory questions (1 × 4-mark question, 1 × 10-mark question, and 3 × 12-mark questions)

→ two essays from a choice of six essay titles, worth 10 and 20 marks respectively

Analysis and evaluation

The table below gives a breakdown of questions that expect you to demonstrate analysis and evaluation in addition to knowledge and application.

Paper	Questions	Additional skills required	Number of marks
1	3 × 6 marks	Analysis	18 marks
	1 × 8 marks	Analysis and evaluation	8 marks
	3 × 12 marks	Analysis and evaluation	36 marks
2	4 × 6 marks	Analysis	24 marks
	2 × 8 marks	Analysis	16 marks
	1 × 10 marks	Analysis and evaluation	10 marks
	1 × 14 marks	Analysis and evaluation	14 marks
3	1 × 10 marks	Analysis and evaluation	10 marks
	3 × 12 marks	Analysis and evaluation	36 marks
	1 × 10 marks	Analysis and evaluation	10 marks
	1 × 20 marks	Analysis and evaluation	20 marks
Total marks			**202 marks out of 240 = 84%**

This table demonstrates the importance of the higher-order skills to your success. Remember, though, that you need to start with key definitions and understanding before you can showcase your analysis and evaluative skills.

WJEC paper structure

The WJEC exams are slightly different from those of the other exam boards in that there are four different papers and candidates are allowed to take Papers 1 and 2 at the end of year 1 of the course if they wish.

The papers

Paper 1: Business opportunities

This paper is 1 hour 15 minutes long. It is worth a total of 60 marks and 15% of the A-level.

This is an AS-style paper, which means that there are fewer longer-response questions. The exam features:

→ a number of case study questions and short-answer responses worth between 2 and 8 marks

→ two slightly longer evaluative questions worth 10 and 12 marks respectively

Paper 2: Business functions

This paper is 2 hours long. It is worth a total of 80 marks and 25% of the A-level.

There are three different compulsory case studies and compulsory questions.

For *each* case study, you are likely to face:

→ two or three data questions (3–4 marks maximum)

→ two or three 6- to 8-mark analyse questions

One of the case study questions will be worth 12 marks and will expect you to evaluate.

Paper 3: Business analysis and strategy

This paper is 2 hours long. It is worth a total of 80 marks and 30% of the A-level.

This paper involves a significant number of short data-response questions from a variety of case studies. This is a very numerical paper with a significant emphasis on calculations. There will be three questions that expect more detailed analysis and evaluation.

Paper 4: Business in a changing world

This paper is 2 hours long. It is worth a total of 80 marks and 30% of the A-level.

This paper involves one case study with five compulsory higher-mark questions (10 marks each) plus two essays from a choice of six essay titles, worth 10 and 20 marks respectively.

Analysis and evaluation

The table on the next page gives a breakdown of questions that expect you to demonstrate analysis and evaluation in addition to knowledge and application.

Paper	Questions	Additional skills required	Number of marks
1	1 × 10 marks	Analysis and evaluation	10 marks
	1 × 12 marks	Analysis and evaluation	12 marks
2	4 × 8 marks	Analysis	32 marks
	1 × 12 marks	Analysis and evaluation	12 marks
3	3 × 10 marks	Analysis and evaluation	30 marks
4	6 × 10 marks	Analysis and evaluation	60 marks
	1 × 20 marks	Analysis and evaluation	20 marks
Total marks			**176 marks out of 300 = 59%**

This table demonstrates the importance of the higher-order skills to your success. Remember, though, that you need to start with key definitions and understanding before you can showcase your analysis and evaluative skills.